Praise for THRIVE and Mike Cook

"*Thrive* is a perfect blend of inspiration and execution and will teach anyone in the workplace how to build great working relationships."

Richard Hadden
Co-author of Contented Cows Give Better Milk

"Mike Cook's focus on "collaborative competence" is perfect for success in today's business environment. Individuals in organizations really get nothing done by themselves; it is collaboration, commitment and passion that make things happen."

Martin Mucci
Chief Operations Officer, Paychex, Inc.

"Anyone attempting to manage work or life needs to pay attention to this book. Mike Cook's message of personal responsibility and adaptability as competitive advantages is pragmatic and powerful."

Lynn Hartrick
CEO,UStec, Inc

"With clear and decisive prose, Mike Cook offers up a compelling view of what's possible for all of us as individual contributors and collaborators in the new world of work."

Marcus S. Robinson, DCH
Founder/Publisher, Ethoschannel.com,
Chairman and Principal Consultant, wetWare, Inc.

"Wow....I'm not the only one wondering where I fit in!"

Gail Cowley
Executive Vice President, Cowley Associates

"...required reading for anyone seeking to thrive, rather simply survive, in today's business environment."

Kathryn Gallant
Research Director, Hall & Partners Healthcare,
New York, NY

"This book is a call to action. It teaches us how to thrive in the new global or "flat world" economy where adaptability is essential. Mike Cook provides a wealth of advice about how to reach one's professional and personal goals. I highly recommend this book."

Thomas L. Campbell, M.D.
William Rocktaschel Professor & Chair, Dept. of Family Medicine, University of Rochester School of Medicine & Dentistry

"This is a "must read" book...memorable, pleasurable, entertaining, direct and thought-provoking. *Thrive* offers a refreshing perspective on the importance of collaboration and adaptability. Cook takes the next step from Thomas Friedman's *The World is Flat*, and proposes what we, the masses, can do next."

Lynne Hambleton
Consultant and Expert on Six Sigma Methodologies

"In America's chilling economic reality, Mike Cook's message is one of optimism and hope. With the wisdom that comes from experience, he walks us through the tenets of workplace transformation. He teaches us how to use the power of interdependence to build an engaged workforce."

Sue Kochan
CEO, brand | cool marketing

"I found myself rereading passages of *Thrive*—not because I didn't "get it" the first time, but because each time, as I delved deeper into the context of my own life experiences, I understood better why I am where I am right now, and where I need to be in the next stage of my career, and for that matter, my life.

Mike Cook uses his amazing ability to simply and logically "peel the onion", methodically uncomplicating a difficult but important concept until it can be understood in a fresh, non-threatening and very personal way."

Jim Cardone
CEO, Warp VII Software

"This important book illuminates the common challenges and fears of being an employee in the global economy, and offers us alternatives to being alienated and powerless. Mike Cook is a penetrating thinker with a practical approach to living and working successfully in our newly flattened world."

Charles Pfeffer
President, Contextus, LLC

"Inspiring and brilliant! Mike shows convincingly that as human beings capable of positive change, when we choose to be adaptable and take personal responsibility for creating value in this knowledge worker age, the benefits to ourselves, the economy and mankind endure beyond words."

Kathleen C. Pringle
President, Predictive Insights, Inc.

"Mike Cook is a genuine trailblazer in organization and team effectiveness. I have had the honor of seeing his theories implemented inside organizations, and the results are truly stunning."

Keating Gore
Senior Consultant,
Organization Development and Change, CGI-AMS

"Many people are talking about the importance of "adaptability." Some are even offering skills in how to be more adaptable. But it's not as simple as that. This book tells us what we need to believe, or stop believing, that would allow us to adaptively succeed in the new workplace. It's a gift to the 21st century worker."

Jim Mahan
Partner and Senior Consultant, Vitalwork

"Michael Cook has a dogged dedication and superb nose for truth. His commitment is to collaborative transformation. With vigorous courage, impeccable humor and the warmest of hearts, Mike's brilliance brings much needed clarification to the questions we all need to be asking ourselves."

Carolyn Cerame
Licensed Therapist

"I am in awe of Mike's clarity of thinking. He captures my experience and, even more importantly, suggests with the use of practices how to be who most of us want to "be" within today's challenging realities."

Shirley Edwards
Consultant and Professional Coach

"During a period of a heavy awakening for American workers, Mike transforms the concept of a global economy with depth and humor and makes it a very personal journey for the reader. Being the spiritual warrior that he is, Mike has taken the very difficult path of facing our workplaces head-on...he shows us a way through to a new possibility."

Deeanne Bevin
Acupuncturist and Doctor of Chinese Medicine

"I've waited a long time for Mike Cook to write a book that reflects his unique personality, philosophy, and inspirational ways. Read *Thrive*—it will enrich your life and help you adapt to the world we live in."

Bruce Miller
Mike's Best Buddy for 45 years

"Insightful...thought provoking...dynamic! The concepts Mike Cook presents transform your thought process. This translates directly to the bottom line of both business and personal life."

Dawn Gerlach
Project Manager, Field Operations, Paychex, Inc.

THRIVE

THRIVE

Standing On Your Own Two Feet in a Borderless World

Mike Cook

PITTSBURGH

Thrive
Standing On Your Own Two Feet in a Borderless World

ISBN-13: 978-0-9767631-5-4
ISBN-10: 0-9767631-5-X

Library of Congress Control Number: 2006927424
CIP information available upon request

First Edition, 2006

St. Lynn's Press, POB 18680, Pittsburgh, PA 15236
412.466.0790 • www.stlynnspress.com

Cover Design – Jeff Nicoll
Book Design – Holly Wensel, NPS
Editor – Catherine Dees

Printed in the United States of America
on recycled paper 🔁

This title and all of St. Lynn's Press books may be
purchased for educational, business, or sales
promotional use. For information please write:
Special Markets Department, St. Lynn's Press, POB 18680,
Pittsburgh, PA 15236

10 9 8 7 6 5 4 3 2 1

Dedication

For my father, Frederick Frances Cook,
and my mother, Margaret Irene Cook,
who never asked me to be anything but myself –

and for Mike Popson and Harry Syring Sr.,
two men who believed in me
when I did not believe in myself.

A Vision for the Future

It is possible to design or find working environments where there is *respect for the individual, regard and reward for original thought, and respect for the right to an inviolable private life.*

Inside such a design or organization, people are empowered in a natural concern for the accomplishment of the organization.

MFC 2/11/90

Table of Contents

Acknowledgments

Most of the ideas and concepts presented in this book have evolved over a period of many years. In that time I have received continuous support and encouragement from my working partners, Jim Mahan, Lisa Bouchard, Kristin Clauss, Elizabeth Fredericks, and my former partner Lynn Hartrick. My working partnership with Jan Cook led to the refinement of the thoughts that eventually became the Design for Engagement that you'll see soon enough.

Keating Gore, Marcus Robinson and Charles Pfeffer have been colleagues and counsel all along the way. The work of the Vitalsmarts Partners—Ron McMillan, Al Switzler, Joseph Grenny and Kerry Patterson—has been a source of inspiration as they forged forward with their commitment to creating a model for dialogue in the workplace. Though I have never met Thomas Friedman, his work, especially *The World is Flat: A Brief History of the 21ˢᵗ Century*, provided the final kick in the pants that spurred me to complete *Thrive*.

As for what you are about to read, there is no doubt that without the guidance of Paul Kelly and the editing partnership of Catherine Dees, both of St.Lynn's Press, you would have tough sledding ahead. Paul Kelly must receive an extra big thank-you for his willingness to bet on this offering when he had many others to choose from. Finally, I lay the primary blame for what I have created here squarely on the shoulders of Pat Jackson, my wife, my partner in life and my muse. She has been a continuous source of enthusiasm and also a counter to my natural excessive tendencies when expressing myself in writing.

I do hope you find *Thrive* to be worth the energy and support all these fine people have provided me as I pursued the refinement of themes that have played in my heart for the last twenty-five years.

Preface

The World Will Never Be the Same...Again

What do you suppose the world looked like to a turnip farmer in central Europe that day in 1570 when Spanish explorer Francisco Pizarro unloaded the first sack of potatoes from Peru (along with all that gold and other treasures)? It was probably like any other day for the turnip farmer, and it remained that way for quite a few years after. The farmer's crop, turnips, was considered the vegetable of nobility, so demand was pretty steady. All he knew or cared to know about that new thing, the potato, was that it was a poor root vegetable, considered food for the lower classes in the Colonies and now being used as cheap fare for hospital inmates on the Continent. In time, the farmer passed on his lands to his sons with the wise counsel that "Turnips is where it's at, don't let anybody tell you any different!"

Then one day in 1780, that farmer's great, great, great, great grandchildren—who continued to pursue the turnip tradition—read in the paper that the Irish had adopted potatoes as a national crop. It turns out that potatoes were found to have some amazing health benefits, but perhaps more importantly, potatoes were easily grown and could produce at a rate that could feed ten people per acre of land. "Interesting news! How nice for the Irish. It's about time they caught a break over there."

For our local turnip farmers, life goes on as it always has; they see no change, they sell their turnips on market day and hear a lot of speculation, which they listen to from a skeptical perspective and return to their farms. Then comes the day when they take their turnips to market and their customers buy less than they had bought before, because now a portion of their budget is being spent on the newly popular potato, the darling vegetable of the health conscious. What was going on?

Unbeknownst to the turnip farmers, a few years earlier, Louis XV had been informed of the health value of potatoes. He decided to launch a potato promotion for his subjects and now potatoes were all the rage in France and rapidly sweeping Europe. That must have been a kick in the head for our turnip-farming friends. Within a short time the turnip was relegated to fodder for livestock. How the mighty had fallen!

Could the farmers have avoided this eventuality? Could they have predicted and prepared for this turn of events? Waiting until they were overrun by potatoes left them unable to respond and with nothing to do except feed those excess turnips to the pigs, if they had any.

The truth is, once the first potatoes arrived in Europe there really was no turning back. It was only a matter of time until someone discovered the value of this South American peasant food. The shift to potatoes was predictable, but only if your focus was on the future. The potato's future did not depend on anything except awareness and imagination—kind of like normalizing trade with China or doing your banking on the Web (remember, even Bill Gates was myopic about the Web).

So, what do you think? Are we in the same position as those turnip farmers, as the world is changing forever again? I am here to say No, we are not! There is plenty of evidence and forewarning to suggest that big changes are occurring, with new rules and new roles in the global economy. Today, the challenge for each of us should be: Will you believe what you see happening and take appropriate action? Are you going to participate with the world as it changes, and if so, how? It's your choice, but you do have to make a choice, and there is risk no matter what you choose. You either get with it or run the big risk of being one of the turnips that gets fed to the pigs.

Helen Keller said,
Security is mostly a superstition; it does not exist in nature, nor do the children of men as a whole experience it. Avoiding danger is no safer in the long run than outright exposure. Life is either a daring adventure or nothing.

We seem to really like that last line. I bet you've seen lots of posters proclaiming "Life is either a daring adventure or it is nothing." I find the full quote to be even more compelling because it exhorts us to take our heads out of the sand and stop hoping for someone (our employers) or something (like our local or national governments) to come to our rescue. Those hopes have little to do with thriving; they are a declaration of helplessness and not very attractive.

Either it is *never* the right time to step up to being responsible for our lives, or it is *always* that time. As you read on you may decide that now is your time. In the final analysis, it is your life and it is your choice.

The only happy people I know are the ones who are working well at something they consider important.

Abraham Maslow

Introduction

Thrive: *verb,* to grow or develop vigorously; to flourish.

Engage: *verb,* to choose to involve oneself in or commit oneself to something, as opposed to remaining aloof or indifferent

Two questions should be on the minds of most people currently in the American workplace: What is it going to take to thrive, not just survive, in what has rapidly become a global economy and an "outsourced" economy? And, is there a formula for thriving?

Thomas Friedman, in his recent book, *The World is Flat: A Brief History of the 21ˢᵗ Century,* identifies four categories of working people who may be untouchable in the economic circumstance that will likely prevail into the foreseeable future:

- The "special people," whose talents are so unique they cannot be duplicated.

- The "specialized people," the architects, the brain surgeons, the software engineers and the like.

- The "anchored people," the barbers, the plumbers, the nurses, the chefs—people whose jobs must be done in a specific location, involving face-to-face contact with a customer.

If Friedman is correct or even in the ballpark—and what he offers seems reasonable to me—I'm wondering where that leaves the rest of us and how many of us there are. To relieve us of total despair he offers a final category that we can inhabit and still be more or less untouchable: He says that if we don't belong to any of these first three categories, then we will simply need to be adaptable. *Adaptable?*

With all due respect to Thomas Friedman, a Pulitzer Prize-winning author, this reminds me of the lame response I gave as I searched for my first jobs after undergraduate school. When various corporate recruiters asked what I was looking for I responded with the voice of the clueless, saying, "Well, I like to work with people." Only after several years in the workplace did I look back at my naïve words and realize that almost any other response would have been made a better impression. *I like to work with people* was vague and hopeful and so very non-specific. Kind of like *adaptable*. While I agree with Mr. Friedman that adaptability is a key to success, as a stand-alone bit of advice it leaves a lot of white space to be filled in. The how-to aspect, in particular. What he does do for us, though, is shine the light of recognition on that portion of the workforce that I'll call "most people." If for no other reason, Friedman's work should be read as a wake-up call for the majority of working citizens in America.

Thrive aims to fill in the white space by offering an approach to being flexible at an individual level, becoming one of Friedman's untouchables—in a word, adaptable. When push comes to shove in a job search, I don't know many of us who wouldn't include in our resume that we are adaptable. So let's get down to work and make it more than a vague and hopeful attribute.

This book is written for "most people," or at least those of us who aspire to be, or to become, adaptable and maintain our value in the outsourced economy. We will consider seriously and delve more deeply into what it really means to be adaptable and what the key elements of adaptability might be. Could adaptability be approached as a practice, perhaps even as a discipline, if we can distinguish its elements? Could we, through conscious and intentional pursuit of the principles of adaptability make ourselves less vulnerable or even at home with the outsourced economy? Could we avoid the historic fate of "most people" who have been vulnerable in the face of technology-driven economic displacement, i.e., getting the traditional "pink slip" and experiencing it like a sucker punch? Could we, in the process of developing adaptability, reclaim a sense of Self and self-confidence that many of us have been asked to (or volunteered to) forfeit when we settled for employment in the first place?

I am about to present what I believe to be the foundational understandings of being truly adaptable. No guarantees, just proven methods that you can choose to use on your own behalf.

My purpose is not to add to your fears; there's enough of that around already. What I'm offering is a remedy for fear—a way out of the self-limiting mindsets that leave us anxious and helpless. We can learn to banish fear, find our own value, and step confidently into our new borderless world. But first we need to understand the big economic picture and how the "old" economy came to be the way it is—and how we ended up thinking it would go on forever.

I do not know everyone and I certainly do not know everything. I have not worked inside every organization. In fact I held a corporate job for only about seven years when

I was in my 20's. The remainder of my adult life I have worked as a consultant doing whatever I could to assist people in reducing the unnecessary suffering we inflict on each other in our places of work. In the process I have also demonstrated to my clients that less suffering leads to improved productivity, leads to greater satisfaction. I don't think this is a tough concept to grasp, but it has not always been an easy sell.

You might ask, "Well, don't most people suffer to some extent at work? Isn't that natural—otherwise why would we call it work?" That depends on how you define "work." There are at least forty different usages of the word in my dictionary, and only a couple of those refer to it as some sort of drudgery. I'm not saying that our work should not be challenging or painful at times. Pain is a part of life; therefore pain is likely a part of work, if not physical then in another form, emotional, spiritual or perhaps psychological. I believe that many things people choose as their work activities will involve obvious pain of some sort. Any professional athlete or welder will tell you that pain is a part of the work they embrace, and these extreme examples only serve to make obvious what is inherent in any pursuit in life.

Pain is certainly a part of a capitalist system. The pain now being experienced by many in our economy—or the fear of pain—is also part of the game and it is not new. Historically, there have been several significant displacements of employment by technology and economic downturn. And historically, those who are displaced cry foul and declare management to be heartless bastards. I am not by any means a management apologist, but I wonder how many times this same basic feature of a capitalist system will recur before we slap our foreheads and say, "Oh! Oh! Now I get it." Maybe that will never happen. That would mean that we have matured as a population and set aside our addiction to security and our sense of entitlement that was born with the industrial revolution and hard-wired by the post-World War II experience. I am not personally optimistic on this score.

Maybe the reason why the pain of displacement always comes with such shock and suffering is that in each of the previous cycles of mass unemployment, a Sacred Cow has been slain in the process.

The first of the herd to go to slaughter was the invincibility of the U.S. economy, thoroughly rendered into ground beef by the Great Depression. That experience turned most people into willing dependents of their employers. Our nation was founded on the myth of rugged individualism, which made heroes of men like Andrew Carnegie, John D. Rockefeller, Leland Stanford and their contemporaries. These men became a standard by which many measured themselves in an age when it seemed like there was no top to the mountain that was the American economy. Then came The Crash, and a nation disillusioned struggled to find a new story that created some certainty. And so, we adopted a new mythology: that politicians created jobs and all economic opportunity resided in the corporate structure. An adult's answer to the uncertainty of life became seeking a good job. By the mid-20th century we had unconsciously collapsed the distinctions between our political and economic systems. Much of the responsibility for individual freedom was subordinated to the seeming security of the corporate structures, and became even more cemented in the robust years of the post-World War II economy. As a nation of workers we sold out to security.

The second sacred bovine to go was "the implied contract" between workers and employers, really only a strange specter resulting from global circumstances in the years 1945-1975. I can still recall as a child growing up, that it was just about as devastating to a family to have a father/husband lose a good job as it was for him to die suddenly. Having a good job did not offer that you'd ever get rich but it did seem to promise that your family would have minimum access to the good life.

The myth of security began to lose its edge when the steel mills started closing in Pittsburgh in the late 70's. There was a snowball effect that followed in the mid-80's as we discovered that all our major industries needed to be "re-engineered." Basically, as a nation and an economy we had grown fat on the post-war feast and it was now time to go on a diet. As we grow older we find that we need to watch what we eat to stay fit. Our economy could not stay fit on the diet of implied promise: If you just worked hard you'd have a job for life. And so we looked for a new story to address the uncertainty of our lives.

The holy heifer that is currently in the chute and next for slaughter has been the lever for politicians since the end of World War I—the protection of nationalism, or the assumed connection between economic security and democracy. This death will be the most painful and bring about more suffering than either of the two preceding it. It also offers the possibility of undermining the stability of the longest running democratic system in history. The stakes are high and it is an ideal time for all of us to step up to acknowledge that we have neglected a basic human responsibility for some time: the essential understanding that each of us owes our community the readiness to provide for our own financial security. And further, until we can provide value to others we ought have no expectation of financial return. Painful words to read? Cold hearted? Maybe, especially if we don't fully understand what "value to others" means. There's a lot we're about to discover about that, and it all comes back to adaptability.

So where do we begin? How do we go about gaining some insight into the principles of adaptability? (Remember, Mr. Friedman created an entire category for this concept.) I believe that an understanding of any circumstance in life begins with an examination of context. For all of us, context represents the operating system within which we each develop our own software. A given operating system will allow many programs to run so long as they are designed consistent with that system. So that is where this book begins.

The first seven chapters are devoted to embracing the current global economic reality and establishing some new approaches that can replace the bankrupt notions that fill our heads with suffering today. The next nine chapters are about gaining competence in adaptability, a process that is more intuitive than a science. A final chapter is written particularly for employers, to help them attract and keep the people they need. Employees might want to take a look, too. There are no secrets here, and everyone should know as much as possible from the widest perspective.

At the end of the book I offer helpful resources and some thoughts on where to go for further development of the competencies I have outlined. Hopefully, by the time you get there you will feel as I do, that the foundation of adaptability, and therefore to thriving in the outsourced economy, is an enhanced level of engagement and appreciation of interdependence. And you can say with me, "While my world may never be the same as it has been, it just might be on its way to being what it was intended to be—a place where there is opportunity for everyone, with no one left out."

I am also hopeful that by the end of the final chapter you will be sufficiently engaged to want to move ahead on your own, and to see to it that others do as well. Perhaps as you do you'll recall the words of Abraham Maslow with which I began: *The only happy people I know are the ones who are working well at something they consider important.* It may be that you have reached the point where something is more compelling, more important to you than simply surviving, and now you are ready to do something about it. Nothing could make me happier, as my primary interest is the promotion of self-sufficiency in a context of interdependence. This may seem a paradoxical statement, but what truth about life is there that is not that way?

One thing I know: You're not going to be doing this standing-on-your-own-two-feet thing alone. You can't, because it has everything to do with you in relationship to others. It is an art and a skill, and it can be yours.

I

Context is Everything

Examining Democracy and Capitalism as
complementary systems with sometimes-conflicting
objectives and a questionable future together

Context: *noun,* the set of circumstances or facts
surrounding a particular event or situation

What you've been hearing: The outsourced economy
has tilted the playing field in favor of equally educated yet largely less expensive workers in other parts of
the world. What you need to know: There is more to this
picture than meets the eye, and it may not be as scary as
it looks.

Trying to find your place in this new economic reality
can be a daunting task. Here in the United States we are
certainly used to competing with each other on our home
turf; competition is a basic pillar of our national self-image.
And even though some of us may have grumbled about
Affirmative Action, in general we have experienced healthy
competition based on a more or less level playing field.

Unlike other periods of economic distress and wide-
spread layoffs—when jobs were disappearing but others

would soon appear in their place—in this economy the jobs are moving to locales where they can be done as well for less money, and they may never return. How unfair is that? I believe that finding ourselves in this apparently unfair situation vis-à-vis the rest of the world is actually more a matter of perspective than immutable truth; and the sooner we come to recognize this the sooner we will be able to develop the perspective and skills needed to thrive in the world as it is, rather than looking backward and wishing for the good old days.

As a consultant on organizational performance for nearly nineteen years, I have worked in every kind of corporate environment, from the very large to the very small. I have had a lot of time to observe what works and what doesn't, and why things go so much better when we understand just a few basic things. It starts with letting go of no-longer-useful concepts about how the world should operate. So, let's first look at the state of the world.

In case you haven't noticed or fully appreciated, democracy and capitalism are spreading. Not everywhere, certainly, but with a huge and increasing global impact economically and politically. Add to this the recent history of our own economy, which has left us more confused than confident about the future, and we have a big problem. It's a problem of context. I believe that "most people" here in the United States are a long way from being sufficiently engaged in the reality of the world we live in now. This lack of full engagement will have adverse consequences for too many of us, while people in other countries are just now getting their first permanent taste of the good life. It's understandable that we're in this predicament, because we as a culture are not tuned to the big picture; there's too much going on right here and now for most of us to keep track of the larger trends taking place in the global arena.

It is hard to fully appreciate something if you can't see it in front of you. These days we can get live coverage

of events around the world: wars, storms, political dem-
onstrations and all the rest. But economies and democra-
cies don't develop in TV time. They can't be understood
in sound bites; they are usually years in the making. So
most people must read about these developments (once
they are already well underway) in Time or Newsweek or
Fortune or Business Week. But the truth is, none of these
popular publications does much in the way of educating
us on a regular basis about global economic development.
And then we're surprised when we wake up one morning
to find that a major shift has happened and it's going to
affect us where we live—quite literally.

I have played my share of competitive sports. I've
been a paying spectator and watched untold numbers of
games on television. So, when I read about the ones I
haven't seen I can pretty well understand what took place,
because I already have the experience required to make my
own reality a reasonable facsimile of what happened on the
playing field far away. But the global economy—that biggest of all games—has largely developed behind a curtain
of silence and invisibility.

There was, of course, that big news when foreign, particularly Japanese, manufacturers began making inroads
into the domestic market for new automobiles. But that
was over thirty years ago, and now those same Japanese
manufacturers (and Koreans and others) actually build
their products in the U.S. and Mexico, employing many
people who formerly worked for U.S. auto manufacturers.
That can't be bad, can it? OK, how healthy does GM seem
to you at the moment, or Ford for that matter?

The absence of directly experiencing the global economy almost assuredly sentences people in America and
many of their children to a future of victimization. Many of
us will eventually ask, if we haven't already, "How did this
happen? Why didn't anyone inform us?" In my view, this is
why books like Thomas Friedman's are so important now.

There is a word I want us to consider: "association," because it has a lot to do with us as Americans, and with what is happening in the world today.

The art of association then becomes...the mother of action, studied and practiced by all.
Alexis de Tocqueville, *Democracy in America, 1835*

When de Tocqueville wrote these words he was describing for his French countrymen and others the uniqueness of the American experiment. He was astounded at the level of what he called "association," both political and otherwise, made possible by the emphasis Americans placed on equality. This emphasis on equality, grounded and maintained by a constitutional form of government, has been the foundation for the preeminence of the United States as a political and economic power on the world stage for nearly two centuries. The world we live in today, with its global economy, is in many ways the product or extension of what de Tocqueville was observing in the 1830's. Hundreds of thousands, no doubt millions, of connections made by people, Americans, from all stations in life for purposes of politics, commerce, and society, have flooded the minds and hearts of people everywhere in the world with ideas of individual freedom and possibility.

The power and possibility of association were simultaneously unleashed on the human race by the signing of the Declaration of Independence. Unconstrained by the previous rules of birth or caste or religious belief, what we are seeing now, as a friend of mine said recently, is the whole world becoming American. You might think that this evolution in the human condition would be a happy occasion for citizens of the United States, the champions of democracy, the defenders of freedom and all the rest. Personally, I am very happy to see the spread of democracy and market economies. People around the globe are now getting opportunities U.S. citizens have had for well over 200 years.

We are no longer #1

What does this foretell for the citizens of the United States? For at least the past hundred years most of us have been so busy "making a living" that we have lost touch with the America de Tocqueville described. We have in many ways foregone the fundamental emphasis on freedom that a system based in equality was designed for, in favor of some form of security, spiritual, economic or political. When de Tocqueville spoke of association he was making both a contextual as well as a literal statement. He was talking about a population—Americans—who, having created the opportunity for personal choice, made use of it in the form of associations never before imagined possible. He was talking about a population that was engaged with *causing* the lives they wanted to live.

Americans today are not "engaged" in the same manner de Tocqueville observed. Since the late 1940's we have as a nation largely benefited from supporting the rebuilding of other economies but at the same time have taken the role of spectator as the other economies developed. It was sort of like we all had a seat in the luxury box owned by the American Franchise. We have developed some of the same myopia as the sports fan who talks about their favorite team as "we." Like these fans of sport, we have grown soft watching the game on the global screen while enjoying the privilege of our inherited status as citizens of the U.S. Unfortunately, like those sports fans who, faced with an increase in ticket prices, always pay up to maintain their fantasy, American citizens may well be soon asked to ante up some of their basic freedoms to maintain the fantasy that we are still #1—and that our government can save us from the risks of the outsourced economy.

We have exchanged much of the spirit of adventure that formed the nation for the security of "jobs" that may or may not give meaning to our lives. If we believe the Gallup organization, their recent studies reveal that less than 30% of us at work are fully engaged with what we have chosen to spend our time on. And political participation is at an all time low. (I chased one of my children and a couple of my younger working associates to the voting booth during the last election.) There are depressingly large numbers of people in their late 20's and early 30's who have never voted. Along with this apathy about politics we're seeing a general trend among Americans towards seeking the assurances and security provided by the larger societal structures. We might note the increasing appeal of the clearly defined rules for living offered by religious fundamentalism.

Americans everywhere, whether at home or in the workplace, are uneasy about their future and do not fully understand why. As I take you through the patterns of my observations I'll do my best to show you ways to confront, reduce, or at least understand your own uneasiness, if you are ready.

2

Saying Goodbye to
the Kings of the Round World

A brief look at global changes that have affected
America's place in the world over the past twenty
years, and a new message for the 21st century

(CNN) March 10, 2005, Microsoft announces that it will
buy virtual office company Groove Networks.

> *And so continued the revolution, unfettered by
> geographic or national borders. Commerce is the
> universal passport; and Capitalism is not bound by
> national borders.*
>
> MFC 4/06/06

It's a Whole New Ballgame

The world is flat again, only this time it's really flat, it's
not just a superstition. Most of the people I know have
been and continue to be directly or indirectly affected by
the accelerating flattening process; "most people" currently in the workplace somewhere in America, that is. What
is the sound of the flat world? It is the man's voice with
an East Indian accent who says his name is Robert on the
other end of the line when you call Travelocity Customer

Service. What does it feel like, this customer service in the flat world? Exactly the same as what we are used to, and in some cases better. A lot of us seem to think there is something wrong with what is happening as jobs move way south and way east, and in some cases way west. If you have any understanding of systems theory there is nothing wrong happening, just a system doing what it was intended to do, finally. Yet, depending on where you are right now on the planet it can feel very wrong, especially if it's your job that just went to India. Robert in Bangalore, working for Travelocity, is feeling pretty good right now. From his perspective the system is working just fine. He loves the outsourced economy.

As individuals, how do we create a framework for understanding and thriving in this new world? First, know that there is nothing wrong. There will be times when it does not feel or look that way. There will be false prophets who will cry that something is wrong and attempt to capitalize on our fears. They will take the form of politicians who make promises for security if we will only relinquish some of our civil freedoms. There will be spiritual impostors who promise a better life if we will just surrender some of our money and a lot of our freedom of thought. You may say that these things have already happened. Our politicians at a national level are preaching fear, and so are many who would have us believe they care about our souls. Little harm has come to the democratic process so far, but that does not mean that our basic freedoms are not at risk. I think they may well be. So again, what about us as individuals? I say the posture we need to take now is one of "being ready," ready for what already has happened and ready for what will soon be happening but may not have yet reached "a theater near you."

There has been a shift in context at a global level. We may eventually wind up winning the global battle for democracy, not so much from the triumph of our ideals as from the more mundane reality that "Everyone wants to be like Mike!" (Remember that one? It was the theme of a not-so-long-ago advertising campaign for Nike's Air Jordan basketball shoes named for the globally recognized Michael Jordan.) Will the eventual propagation of democracy through pragmatic motives be any less satisfying than if it had happened as ours did originally? I cannot say for sure, but for citizens in the U.S. it may seem a bit hollow, since it will bring with it economic adjustments and risk that most people alive today have not experienced.

> *Trade is the natural enemy of all violent passions.*
> *Trade loves moderation, delights in compromise, and*
> *is most careful to avoid anger. It is patient, supple,*
> *and insinuating, only resorting to extreme measures*
> *in cases of absolute necessity. Trade makes men*
> *independent of one another and gives them a high*
> *idea of their personal importance: it leads them to*
> *want to manage their own affairs and teaches them*
> *to succeed therein. Hence it makes them inclined to*
> *liberty but disinclined to revolution.*
>
> Alexis de Tocqueville, *Democracy in America*

These global economic and democratic changes—and the inevitable adjustments and risks—will only accelerate for some time to come; ironically, here in the U.S. we will get another opportunity to determine just how committed we are to a democratic form of government and the individual freedoms it provides.

I am reminded of my experience with Hurricane Frederick in 1979, when I got a big lesson about adjustments and risks. I lived in Pascagoula, Mississippi, and worked at the local refinery. I had moved to the area a year earlier from the West Coast and was just getting used to the humidity after fifteen months. I came into work the morning of the storm, a bright sunny day with puffy clouds.

When I arrived at my office I found a scribbled note telling me to get to the main conference room as soon as I could. There, I found the majority of the refinery's senior managers crammed tightly into the room and there were big maps all over the walls. I quickly found out that we were well into hurricane preparations; in fact they had begun during the night. It was a hard situation to comprehend for someone who had never experienced such a storm. The sun was shining, the breeze blew softly through the windows but the air inside that conference room was tense with anticipation. I looked outside; activity had picked up in the refinery as well. Sand was being bagged, reserve compressors were being raised on stilts and there was a buzz about the whole place. These people had done this before!

As I took my place in the room I asked one of the more seasoned people to explain what was happening and why the tension was so palpable. He said that what I was seeing had over time become standard procedure, unfortunately from lessons learned the hard way. What the people there had learned was that preparation for the storm had to begin well before you could see any evidence of danger. A refinery is designed to run 24 hours a day, 365 days a year and they rarely shut down, as the economics would be prohibitive. Experience had led to the understanding that if preparations had not begun by the time the storm was within a certain distance of landfall, the consequences could be much more severe than would be realized by those couple of days of lost production. I guess it was maybe three hours after I arrived when the sky began to darken and the wind rapidly picked up. The storm was predicted to reach landfall about thirty miles to our east but we were going to get plenty of rain and wind. We listened continuously to the national weather service channel; then, just about at the point where the storm would touch land it veered sharply to the west and passed over our plant, eye and all! There was damage to the plant, what you might expect from lots of wind and rain but nothing like what would have occurred had the preparations not been made. And I got to see the eye of a hurricane.

What's my point? The folks at the refinery could have gambled, they could have relied on the weather service predictions as a guarantee of safety and made minimal preparation. They could have been hard headed and opted to stay in production rather than take the loss of product. As it turned out they made the best choice possible; they had planned for the worst and the worst showed up. The refinery did not escape some negative consequences but we minimized them by collaborating with the circumstances. We embraced the interdependence between nature and economy.

We were winners in a game that was rigged!

Some years back I had a conversation with one of my younger associates. I was about forty-five then and he was maybe thirty. He was talking to me about his plans for the future and how he hoped he would have what it took to be successful, etc. I looked at him and said, "You do realize the game is rigged don't you?" He looked at me strangely and asked for explanation. I told him there was nothing inherently bad about a game being rigged so long as everyone knows it's rigged. What's not good is when it's rigged, many people know it, and nobody owns up to it. First off, I said, the game was designed by white males who I believe consciously or unconsciously rigged the game in their favor. That may not be all that surprising given the fact of the white maleness of the Founding Fathers, the brilliance of these men and the cultural norms at the time of the country's formation. These were some of the most astute political minds the world has ever seen come together in one place. And they had something few men possessed: inspired foresight. With the Declaration of Independence and the Bill of Rights I think the Founding

Fathers knew full well what they were unleashing on their world.

The years since the nation's founding have seen the progression, not always steady, of the unwinding of the original game's rigging as we have seen civil rights extended to more and more groups. Those documents set in place the "time release of liberty." My young associate thought for a moment, then asked if that was all. Oh no, I said to him, there was another kind of rigging already in place. On the economic side the rigging was provided by the distance across both the Atlantic and Pacific that allowed our economy to develop pretty much in isolation at first, and then as industrialization blossomed, the successive wars in Europe, Japan and southern Asia gave us access to new markets— and another decided economic advantage. Those wars not being in our country, our factories were not bombed, nor our railways torn up. Once armed conflict ceased, the U.S. was ready to quickly switch back to commercial production and fill the backlog of demand for consumer goods created by war shortages. Don't forget, our economy was making a very slow recovery from the crash of 1929 when World War II came along, giving us a powerful economic boost and then an advantage as we emerged from the war with the one economy that could operate at full capacity. It took the rest of the world nearly forty years to rebuild after the War.

"What about now?" my friend asked. "How are things rigged now?" My response was based solely on my own experience, so I'm always open to questions. How is the game rigged now? I told him that whether we like to admit it or not, a lot of the initial rigging is still in place. Opportunities are indeed more plentiful for women and minorities than they were when the country started. It is a trend that will continue; yet at the same time, if you happen to be a white male with reasonable intelligence and some ambition there is still a sufficient advantage—and in my view not much of an excuse for not being at least modestly successful in the United States. My young associate then admitted that he knew in his heart what I was saying was correct and he should at a minimum be grateful for having won the gene pool lottery.

The same cannot be said for the U.S. economy or the U.S. standard of living. The advantage we experienced following World War II will likely never be repeated in history. As Thomas Friedman points out to us, it is far less likely for global business partners to allow warfare to disrupt the economic interests once they have realized the mutual benefits of interdependence as part of a global supply chain. This being the case, the rules of capitalism are now in full swing on the planet. The dominant context for human beings everywhere has become the pursuit of freedom. Much of the world now recognizes that democracy is not just a good political system, it is also a great underpinning for a capitalistic economic development. First, the fall of the Soviet Union, and then recently the engagement of the Chinese people in hot pursuit of the good life, have heralded a tipping point for democracy. It is likely to be a messy process, getting to anything resembling what our Founders envisioned—and there will always be resistance from those who like their power neat and centralized. For those nations where democracy has yet to be embraced there is no longer a choice; there is inevitability. Embrace democracy, even in a limited form, or be forever shut out as a nation from the global marketplace.

So how do we shake the memories of our glorious past? I am writing this book for those people among "most people" who are ready to ride the hurricane that is the global economy; those people who are willing to act as a partner to the global economy while remaining a citizen of the United States, committed to a democratic form of government. This group of people will be formed by self-nomination. It is open to anyone willing to step up to the responsibility of being a player instead of a spectator. But, in order to truly enjoy the experience of the newly flattened globe, members of the group will need to count on being adaptable. They will be the ones who recognize and embrace collaborative skills as fundamental elements of adaptability.

3

Standing on Your Own Two Feet: Choosing Freedom over Dependence

Is there a relationship between civic freedom
and economic freedom? Not only is there
a relationship, there is an interdependence.

*I must say a word about fear. It is life's only true
opponent. Only fear can defeat life...You dismiss
your last allies: hope and trust. There, you've
defeated yourself. Fear, which is but an impression,
has triumphed over you.*

Pi in *Life of Pi*, Yann Martel

Fear is No Longer Affordable

Some years ago Edwards Deming offered us a landmark
management book, *Out of the Crisis*. In this classic of
management theory Deming put forth his famous Fourteen Point System for establishing the sustainability of an
enterprise. *Out of the Crisis* is an awkward book, yet its
power is difficult to deny. In many ways it was sort of the
business version of the Ten Commandments. Unfortunately, as such it has been given the same "pick and choose"
treatment as the Commandments and never been adopted

whole cloth by business leaders, at least here in the U.S. Maybe it is something about the American spirit, maybe it is something about the pragmatism of business leaders. The fact remains that the Fourteen Point System has never been fully implemented. I offer them here so that you can see the foundations of a healthy working environment—for the employed, for management, and ultimately, for the business itself.

Deming's Fourteen Points

- Create constancy of purpose for the improvement of product and service, with the aim to become competitive, stay in business, and provide jobs.

- Adopt a new philosophy of cooperation (win-win) in which everybody wins and put it into practice by teaching it to employees, customers and suppliers.

- Cease dependence on mass inspection to achieve quality. Instead, improve the process and build quality into the product in the first place.

- End the practice of awarding business on the basis of price tag alone. Instead, minimize total cost in the long run. Move toward a single supplier for any one item, based on a long-term relationship of loyalty and trust.

- Improve constantly, and forever, the system of production, service, planning, of any activity. This will improve quality and productivity and thus constantly decrease costs.

- Institute training for skills.

- Adopt and institute leadership for the management of people, recognizing their different abilities, capabilities, and aspiration. The aim of leadership should be to help people, machines, and gadgets do a better job. Leadership of management is in need of overhaul, as well as leadership of production workers.

- Drive out fear and build trust so that everyone can work more effectively.

- Break down barriers between departments. Abolish competition and build a win-win system of cooperation within the organization. People in research, design, sales, and production must work as a team to foresee problems of production and use that might be encountered with the product or service.

- Eliminate slogans, exhortations, and targets asking for zero defects or new levels of productivity. Such exhortations only create adversarial relationships, as the bulk of the causes of low quality and low productivity belong to the system and thus lie beyond the power of the work force.

- Eliminate numerical goals, numerical quotas and management by objectives. Substitute leadership.

- Remove barriers that rob people of joy in their work. This will mean abolishing the annual rating or merit system that ranks people and creates competition and conflict.

- Institute a vigorous program of education and self-improvement.

- Put everybody in the company to work to accomplish the transformation. The transformation is everybody's job.

Now think about where you are employed. How close is that environment to what Deming suggests as optimum?

I hope you're among the lucky few. If most of those fourteen points haven't been fully implemented as part of your work culture, why is that? Are there actions you could take, requests you could make, conversations you could initiate to stimulate energies that would move your environment in the direction Deming recommends? These are questions that go right in the same box as "Why don't our places of work more closely reflect the democratic principles upon which our nation was built?" The answer to either question may be the answer to both. You don't have to get real creative to see the application of these fourteen principles at a societal level, give or take a few tweaks.

I'll conjecture that the primary failing of Americans is also their greatest strength: pragmatism. We are a predominantly practical people with little tolerance for the intangible. When we cannot see the immediate usefulness of an idea we tend to dismiss it offhandedly as "not being practical" or "too soft" or "unrealistic." We have little fundamental regard for or facility with *the power of context*. Consequently, somewhere along the line Deming's system turned into a set of tools for problem solving, rather than remaining the basis for *a way of doing business* that Deming intended.

The cynical might offer that our behavior is typically American, the skeptic might suggest that the quality movement was never about quality anyway. The pragmatist might fill in with, "Well, you have to pick and choose; you can't do everything." I prefer a more altruistic view, one that suggests that we are still early in the process of understanding what Deming was driving at, and we are still early in the experimentation with democracy. Deming believed that the purpose of a business was to produce an optimum amount of value for the optimum number of people for as long as possible!

> **Optimum:** *noun,* the amount or degree of
> something that is most favorable to some end.

Americans don't do "optimum," we do maximum, and Deming knew that maximum was not sustainable. We "super size;" Deming was for "right size." He was not only a proponent of quality in manufacturing; he was in favor of quality of life. His fourteen points were a philosophy, for manufacturing certainly, but also for living in a capitalist system.

So then, where are we with this philosophy? I'd say we are at the point where we get to confront the parts we didn't understand at first glance. With both democracy and the philosophy of Edwards Deming we are at a "pragmatic juncture." We have used all that our understanding of democracy and our understanding of capitalism have allowed, and now we have reached the place, maybe some time ago, that will be the most difficult for all of us to fully embrace: Driving fear from the workplace. Deming addressed this point in terms of management practices. Most often when questions of fear are written about or addressed, management is considered both the source and the cure. I say the problem runs deeper; it runs to the psyche of each of us, perhaps most especially to the psyche of those of us who are conscious enough to even consider responsibility for the issue.

It is in the relationship called "employment" that the problem originates. The problem is of course that we come to work already fearful. Managements may leverage our fear but unless we can be scared they cannot even do that.

Almost all of us recognize the necessity of finding something to do that allows us to take care of ourselves economically. Those of us who make the attempt generally succeed, some more than others. Unfortunately, a vast number of us do not accomplish much more than this. We may find a way to meet or exceed our economic needs, but rarely do we find a calling for ourselves, a pursuit that provides us the opportunity to know what we are fully capable of, what we will completely engage with—what will return to us something money will never buy, a sense of confidence and a freedom. The difference between those of us who do and those who don't? I think it may come down to two things: vision and responsibility. The two are difficult to separate. Vision without responsibility is merely daydreaming. Responsibility without vision is ungrounded and likely devolves into something like obligation. I am going to proceed on this premise for the sake of the dialogue that follows.

> *Vision is where tomorrow begins, for it expresses what you and others who share the vision will be working hard to create. Since most people don't take the time to think systematically about the future, those who do, and who base their strategies and actions on their visions, have inordinate power to shape the future.*
>
> Burt Nanus

I am less interested in the secrets of success than I am in the secrets of living a fearless life. When I connect the basic concept of political freedom with economic freedom rooted in personal responsibility—rather than rugged individualism—I become inspired. I cannot escape the idea that there are choices to be made, for me in my life, for you as well, and for us as a nation. To go forward from this point with the experiment begun over 230 years ago does not seem much of a stretch. In the history of civilizations ours is still an adolescent.

But we can grow up, and we must grow up together. How will we be able to tell that we are on the path to growing up as a people? Here is one man's optimistic view:

> *You've learned the arts of mutual dependence, learned that we achieve full humanity in a web of mutual commitments. You know how to give and receive love without exploiting those you love or are loved by. You take turn at nurturing and let yourself need others. You recognize that all of the many kinds and varieties of loving relationships involve reaching out, accommodating, communicating, accepting vulnerability and much more.*
>
> John W. Gardner

I have read these words from John W. Gardner many times over and I cannot help thinking that this could be our maxim, whether as individuals or nations. Gardner was not a clergyman, he was not a philosopher, not in the traditional sense. He was a statesman, a role that has a lot of vacancies these days. He worked for five different presidents as a cabinet member or an advisor, without regard to whether they were Republican or Democrat. He worked for the win-win solutions, he worked for America. When he spoke of love it was not hearts-and-flowers love. His was a love based on mutuality of purpose, respect and understanding. His was a grown-up love.

As we go through our younger years, especially our teenage years, we dream of a day when we can live the freedom we believe we see in the lives of those older than us. Then, as we move out into the world we rapidly discover that there were facts and realities that had not been obvious. These freedoms we desired were not so free. In fact they were downright expensive. Many of us plotted a course that I'll call "faux independence." The term fits well for me as I observe many people who live as though they have "grown up;" they have homes, cars, families. They take vacations, they go out to eat, they pick their own movies, they have opinions. On the surface they may feel in control of their lives, but there are unintended consequences and suffering when their adult lives fail to deliver on the promise they saw as children. Without intending to, a great number of us made a deal with the devil, a deal that will haunt us throughout adulthood. We have become addicts without chemical dependency. We are addicted to security, the kind of subtle, creeping security that gradually robs us of our own power to fulfill a life in all its promise.

This chapter is designed to support you in becoming an advocate for yourself, standing on your own two feet. I do not mean you *should* stand on your own two feet; I mean you *can and must*. I have limited concern for what you should do as long as you don't crowd me. I am really only concerned with your developing power—personal power, to be more specific. Personal power arises from making choices and true choices demand responsibility and vision. We will never see the full fruition of democracy until each of us knows we are powerful. The world will not be safe for the full expression of capitalism until each of us experiences our own power. I am in favor of both, but when I look around me I see an unwillingness to fully acknowledge the interdependence that underlies our entire existence—the interdependence that would provide us the greatest access to the freedoms we so desperately imitate in our lives and our international politics.

Consider this carefully: What passes for freedom in much of our culture is really privilege purchased by the economically successful. What passes for security in much of our culture and our places of work is really silent victimization. The unwillingness to acknowledge our interdependencies has sentenced us to lives of imitated and purchased freedoms on a material plane, rather than the experience of freedom, with or without the material trappings.

Please keep in mind that I did not say anything about standing on your own two feet alone. That's what we already do and it has left us operating in a constant state of low-grade terror. Standing on your own two feet is about us growing up together, at work and as citizens. The world of work has changed, on that we all agree. The world of opportunity may now be changing even faster. Let me share a little story.

My father worked for the same small electrical contracting company for thirty years. Over that period the world he operated in was very stable. If there was any illusion of instability it was only that in our town sometimes business was brisk and sometimes it was slow, but there was always business. My father was a very conscientious part of the little company and his dealings with other firms gained him a reputation for being steady and reliable, in those days two of the most desirable traits for any worker. Over the years he was approached by several other firms to take positions with them, with advancement opportunities and a better standard of living for our family. He never even seriously considered those options, saying that the little firm had been very good to him and he owed them his loyalty. In my teenage years I challenged him on this topic a number of times, encouraging him to think of himself or at least his family before he deferred to loyalty... to no avail.

One day, after these thirty years of loyal service he was informed quite out of the blue that his services were no longer needed and he was going to be replaced by one of the owner's sons! My mother called me that day to let me know and asked me to talk to my dad because she was concerned for his mental state. I reached him late in the day, concerned as well, to see if there was anything I could offer by way of comfort. He answered the phone in far too jolly a mood as far as I was concerned, and I thought perhaps he had spent the afternoon in some bar. What I found instead was a man who had taken himself through an amazing emotional and psychological journey in a period of a few hours. He told me that when he received his notice he was stunned and left the office almost immediately. He drove around aimlessly for a long time, feeling sorry for himself, enraged at the injustice of this action, wondering how he could have been such a fool—and on and on, in that sort of mental swirl that you can identify with if you have ever had a very nasty surprise.

After a few hours of this he said he suddenly got tired of his own reaction to the situation; it was wearing him out. He thought through all the years, thought about all he had done with and for the little electrical firm, and came to the realization that the fate of that business which he had devoted his life to was no longer his problem. In a flash of clarity he came to see that his future was in his own hands; for the first time in thirty years he didn't have the burden of loyalty. He had dozens of friends and even more acquaintances; surely there would be some economic benefit to having been so friendly and outgoing all those years. He could focus his attention on what he wanted to do and what would be best for his family, and see what was possible.

The rest is a happy history of my father, at fifty-eight, beginning his own on-his-feet career. For a time he hired out his services as a very competent shade-tree electrician, first around the neighborhood and then to others around town who were aware of the quality of his work. He was as busy as he wanted to be and making better money than he ever had as an employee of the electrical firm. When he turned sixty-five he activated his pension option, finding that he had weathered seven years on his own just fine. But he missed the contact of being part of something, so he looked around and found himself a full time position with a small specialty luggage and gift store that was struggling to stay afloat.

He has been there for the past eighteen years repairing broken luggage and making people smile, and at eighty-three has no interest in being retired, if that meant not having a reason to get up in the morning, a place to contribute, people to interact with. As I said, the little store struggles, sometimes my father gets paid on time and sometimes he doesn't, but he always gets what he is there for, which is obviously not the money.

So what about the notion of "choosing" that I began with? My father recognized, in the midst of what was apparent chaos in his life at a very inopportune time, that he had a choice. He didn't have a choice about what had happened, he had a choice about what he would make of it and he chose to be the author of his own life. He could have picked victim, in fact for a short period of several hours he did choose victim. By contrast, my mother has never forgiven the man who let my father go, or his children. She wouldn't even go to the man's funeral when he passed on two years ago, while my father had spent hours with him in the hospital prior to his death.

This is what I mean about choosing. In the space of a few hours my father reorganized a fifty-eight-year history based on dependency, created a vision for himself and set out to responsibly execute it. Perhaps it seems trite or too obvious, but this suggests that many of the most important lessons of life involve *learning what we already know*. This is one example; it is imperative to the question of being a standing on your own two feet kind of person that it get answered in the early going, or you can spend a lot of time looking over your shoulder for when it's all going to be OK again.

You may have already had an experience similar to my father's and still not have adopted the standing-on-your-own-two-feet mindset, meaning you are still in danger of being as much a victim as anyone else.

The events of our lives do not determine the way we see or feel about what has occurred. The facts of the situation are also not the determinant. I have sat listening to Ph.D. corporate researchers whine about their companies' insistence that they work on something other than what they were personally curious about— "You're asking us to do something that could be commercialized! Not fair!" Put in a position of being called upon to demonstrate their economic value, these folks wanted to argue for a past situation—for the status quo, for things as they've always been. Their ox was being gored and they didn't like it. Even though they had the advantage of having credentials that could earn them significant income elsewhere, their conversations bore a strong resemblance to ones I have had with out-of-work steel workers in Pittsburgh in the early 80's. "We put in all that time, how could they have done this to us?" Again, my friends, a reminder that time served and loyalty are not the currency of the new economy.

A wonderful mentor of mine, Dan Sullivan, creator of The Strategic Coach, an entrepreneurial program for business owners, does a much better job of mocking this mindset than I do; but he also has something very important to say on the topic. He has come up with what he considers the individual's declaration of independence for this new economy. He calls it the "entrepreneurial declaration" (I'm quoting from my notes of his presentation, which means I'm probably paraphrasing a few words):

"I am now and forever solely responsible for my own financial welfare. I shall expect no return in life until I have first delivered value to another."

In his view, and I concur, each one of us must develop the mindset of an entrepreneur. Not that we need to become entrepreneurs, rather that we see the world through entrepreneurial eyes. Sullivan suggests that the entrepreneurial perspective is one that expects no economic return until value is produced for another party. He is not talking about the "doing" of an entrepreneur, but the "being" of an entrepreneur.

This is much more than a simple concept, it sets the stage for a fundamental shift in the way we see the world around us. It illuminates the means by which we set ourselves free economically. Taken seriously, it is the doorway into the world of a self-managed life. The circumstance of being let go in some corporate downsizing action does not set you free or leave you standing on your own two feet. It leaves you unemployed and standing in the street! Nor does moving from position to position as money and options are waved in your face indicate a state of freedom and self-dependence. You can still be a victim of the next set of circumstances or be acting as an economic whore or a New Age brat taking advantage of circumstances you had nothing to do with creating—as with the huge demand for talent in information technology in the late 1990's. "Standing on your own two feet" is a context, it is a *possibility*, even if you have the same position or work with the same company you have been with for twenty-five years. I am talking about **choice, not circumstance**. As someone possessed of highly sought-after skills you can be just as much a victim of a secure situation as the person who is hanging on hoping that the next Reduction in Force doesn't sweep them into the street.

Having made the entrepreneurial declaration, as seriously as anyone can say anything, and understanding its implications, the "stand-up guys" begin to see the world around them differently. It is no less risky to adopt the mindset of standing on your own two feet than it is to continue on the path of the willing dependent; however, in the case of the former, a person begins to experience personal power. They see themselves as creator of the risk rather than victim. They begin to see themselves as essentially and undeniably interconnected with the people around them, and they recognize that the key to power is to deliver value *before* expecting return—a very different perspective.

It's kind of like getting a really good understanding of gravity. Once this takes place you are far less likely to leave a building by a third floor window, but if by chance this should occur you are probably more prepared to deal with the consequences and get back in action quickly... well, metaphorically speaking, that is!

Another brief story may help to clarify my point. Recently I received a phone call from a very distraught close friend. She had worked within one of the best-known companies in the world for about fifteen years, performed well, been rewarded but always had the question of whether she was really appreciated or if she had what it took to make it out there in this new world of opportunity. Out of the blue, she was contacted and wooed by another best-known company in the world. In a swirl of activity in a very short period she was offered a 50% increase in salary, a $15K signing bonus and an opportunity to do some exciting work. Within a matter of weeks she was gone to the new position. She was very proud of the new deal, even though it meant she had to move half way across the country; she was finally cashing in with options, to boot.

So I get this phone call after about six months and she is miserable in the new company—"It's just like the other place!" In addition, she is away from her twenty-something daughter and her gentleman friend and her other friends she has cultivated over the past fifteen years. "I thought I was a together enough person to make this move," she says to me on the phone, "maybe I just can't cut it after all." After a moment's thought I replied, "Perhaps the way you are feeling has nothing to do with whether you are together, maybe it's an indicator that you just didn't realize what was most important to you, and being away has helped you get clear about that." My comment stopped her mental gear-grinding and she thanked me and promised to see me soon.

My friend did not know she was a "willing dependent." She has been a single mother, successful team player and leader for many years where she was formerly employed. She had moved her career ahead successfully on several occasions by advocating for herself and building a track record of performance, but she was never able to affirm her own value for herself. It always took some form of outside approval to make her world OK.

In the midst of all this success she was smitten by the whirlwind courtship of another firm and, not being completely grounded in her own value, had made a mistake. Because she now understands what's important to her and her own value in the world, she sees that this is correctable. I like the phrase, "You pays your money, you takes your chances" as it applies here. My friend was unwittingly playing with her own "gravity" and didn't know it until she fell out the window and hit the ground.

Let's move on now from that single most important mental/emotional shift, the personal declaration of standing on your own two feet—and head into how to prepare yourself once you have decided to make the journey. I should warn you that it is not independence you will be seeking, but the freedom to be who you are. The "who you are" I am referring to here is, in the most literal sense, a fully functioning human being. If you find this freedom, I think you will also find that fundamental to being this type of being, is a desire to be part of something with other humans, *a place to belong*, a sense of real congruity between yourself and your working environment—just as my father did when he went to work for that little luggage shop.

Now I want to give you another word definition: **Dharma**. It is a Sanskrit term with many layers of interpretations, but for our purposes dharma means living in a way that is true to your own highest spirit, true to your *being*. Dharma is your inner spiritual reference point for your choices. To live dharmically is to be in harmony with your true self ("who you are"). I think that's what my dad's life is about. I wish this for everyone, in whatever way it manifests itself in your lives

4

Don't Lead a Stupid Life

What developing a life purpose, personal mission and work mission have to do with choosing a workplace

The higher nature in man always seeks for something which transcends itself and yet is its deepest truth; which claims all its sacrifice, yet makes this sacrifice its own recompense. This is man's dharma, man's religion, and man's self is the vessel.

Rabindranath Tagore

I'm sure you know by now that I try to keep things pretty bottom line. In my work with clients I often give my own very simplistic observation of what the process of life comes down to. So here it is: You are born, you grow up in your parents' care, you stay in your parents' house for as long as it makes sense or as long as they will put up with you, you go out into the world, find something you love to do with people you love doing it with, you do that for as long as that is mutually beneficial and satisfying and then you die. I am open to the idea that there are some variations on this overall scenario, but they pretty much wind up the same. So if this is really the deal, then life must be about the journey, since all the stories have the same ending. That being the case, we'd be best advised to be awake for the journey, because it is the only thing we really have to work with.

Unfortunately, many of us pick our way through life in a stupefied state. We think of life as a problem to be solved when there is no solving it. Is there a different way to approach or consider life? For centuries, philosophers and great spiritual leaders have brought us to one central theme: If there is a "solution to life" it lies in the creation of a purpose.

What is my purpose in life, what is my responsibility? Whether I like it or not, I am on this planet, and it is far better to do something for humanity. So you see that compassion is the seed or basis. If we take care to foster compassion, we will see that it brings the other good human qualities. The topic of compassion is not at all religious business; it is very important to know that it is human business, that it is a question of human survival that is not a question of human luxury. I might say that religion is a kind of luxury. If you have religion, that is good. But it is clear that even without religion we can manage. However, without these basic human qualities we cannot survive. It is a question of our own peace and mental stability.
The Dalai Lama, from *A Policy of Kindness: An Anthology of Writings By and About the Dalai Lama,* compiled and edited by Sidney Piburn

Whether a purpose for life is there in fact, or is a matter of personal construction is of little consequence to me. What matters is the investment you make in making it your own. I try to be careful with the words I pick, and I chose **stupid** in this chapter title very carefully, not to signify ignorance but to indicate a state of awareness—or perhaps more precisely, a state of unawareness.

Stupid: *adjective,* dulled in feeling or sensation

I have had the good fortune to have many fine teachers in my life; maybe you have as well. Of all the many things I have been taught, the single most beneficial one in helping me see the journey is the notion that, left to our own devices, it is very easy to go through life in a condition of stupor.

This is not a character defect or a function of intelligence, but it is a terminal condition, in that we can maintain this stupid state indefinitely, all the way to the end of the journey. I know you know what I am talking about because we can see this in others, but usually not ourselves. The state of stupor comes about through lack of understanding how the experience of one's life is created—not knowing that there may be a difference between the way one sees the world and what is actually happening.

I just recently came from a meeting with a close friend. He had the day before returned from a vacation in a very exclusive enclave. He had been looking forward to that opportunity for some time and I was expecting to be regaled with stories of the comfort and privilege he had experienced. Instead, my friend told me that he felt as though he had not been on vacation at all. How could that be? I asked him. I thought that area was supposed to be Nirvana for Americans of means. His reply was not all that surprising because I know my friend well, and know that he has been on a spiritual journey himself for some years. "Everything was perfect," he said, "there were beautiful homes, beautiful people, and beautiful places to eat and play golf, and it was like walking through a dream state." He found that for all the perfection it felt lifeless. Everything that was living was carefully controlled and looked the way it was "supposed to look." "It was like spending six days in the 'Stepford Resort'," he laughed. "I was looking for a place to really relax and slow down, but this place went beyond slowing down; there was no pace at all and every day was the same as the one before. It was completely predictable and completely boring. Worst of all, I had thought for years that was what I should be shooting for. I said dream state, I should have said nightmare! It was frightening—like life was over and now what was ahead was simply existing in a state of stupor. And I still feel like I need a vacation!"

Don't think that I am promoting the notion that less is better; that was not the point of my friend's or this story. It was to underscore the challenge of living our lives in a state of awareness. Americans live in a culture that seems to idolize the notion of wealth for its own sake. This is not new for us; it is at least as old as the nation itself.

That famous early observer of America, Alexis de Tocqueville had more to say about his early impressions of Americans during his first visit here in 1831. He admired us for many aspects of our national character, but others left him puzzled:

> *As one digs deeper into the national character of the Americans, one sees that they have sought the value of everything in this world only in the answer to this single question: how much money will it bring in?*
> Alexis de Tocqueville, Democracy in America, 1835

Can we say that he got us all wrong? Or did he see a tendency we need to examine? Money and its privileges are outside ourselves; therefore they cannot be our purpose. They can be goals. Yet, as my friend confronted on his vacation, the goal—whether it is money or anything else—is not the important thing; it is part of the process of fulfilling a self-created purpose. Without purpose the goal of affluence, like any other goal, is hollow and deadening to our spirit. For me, being awake is a matter of constant need for vigilance.

It is not just affluence or the pursuit of affluence that has a seductive yet unrewarding outcome. Often times in my work with clients I ask them the question, "Would you like to be right, or would you like to be rich?" You'd be surprised at the long silences that follow. It is at once a simple question and the beginning place for a powerful inquiry into what you are up to—not only in life as a whole, but what you are up to in life, moment to moment.

Returning to the problem of not leading a stupid life, I have another story. It has to do with the difference between what you think you see and what is really going on. Not that long ago my oldest sister met a man she thought would be the right guy to marry. She had had a horrific first marriage that lasted far too long in the opinion of the family, and it had been several years since she had shown any real interest in anyone new. One thing was certain, at least for the family: My sister could not be trusted when it came to picking husband material. Maybe you have someone in your family like this? Anyway, she brought this guy home to meet everyone, and from the get-go my mother treated him with great disrespect. (I know you don't know my mother, but she is far from subtle, and she has the ferocity of a mother lion if she thinks one of her cubs is threatened.) This goes on for a while, and the rest of us get to know this guy. He passes muster with us, but it doesn't get any better with Mom. After about six months of bringing him over to the house and having my mother spend the whole time being nasty, my sister finally tells Mom she is going to marry this man. She also will not return to my parents' home until things changed when her man is there. I'm telling this without your having the full benefit of the phone calls from my mother continually re-affirming that my sister had terrible judgment in men, this guy was no different, she was about to make another terrible mistake, yadda, yadda, yadda...

Around this time I made a visit home to see the folks, expecting to get an earful about this, since it had been going on for quite a while, and knowing that my mother doesn't respond well to ultimatums. When I arrived, braced for the worst, I found her in the midst of helping my sister plan for the wedding! What happened? I asked my mother after my sister had left. Where was all the venom?

She said that when my sister told her that she was definitely going to marry this man and wasn't going to put up with Mom's attitude or behavior any longer, it forced her to examine exactly why she was so adamant about the situation. What she saw was that she had suffered deeply with my sister through her first marriage and she was determined to protect her from ever having a similar experience, so much so that she was on the verge of having that fear cost her the relationship with her daughter. When she saw what she was doing it was clear to her that she wasn't willing to lose her daughter, under any circumstances. I asked her if she had given in to the situation and she said no, she just changed her mind.

This story has a happy ending. The marriage has been very successful and my mother now loves the guy. But what about the notion of my mom changing her mind? She said she could see that her fear for my sister's welfare and the pain that she experienced had so shaped her perspective that she couldn't tell the difference between what she thought she was seeing and what was happening, no matter what the rest of the family tried to show her. But why now? She told me that somehow, in the midst of her fury over the situation she suddenly saw that her point of view was simply that, a point of view, and it had become too costly to maintain. She also saw that from the perspective of her "purpose," the goal of protecting herself and my sister from another painful experience, had superceded her true purpose, which was the happiness of her children. She was meeting her *goal* by protecting my sister, yet at the same time failing to fulfill her *purpose*.

There is an unfortunate theme in this story of my mother, and I have heard it repeated many times when people tell of events that led them to make major revisions in their lives: Pain—many times accompanying personal tragedy—is often the stimulus for a change in the direction of our lives. I know you know this, but it never hurts to remind ourselves from time to time.

I was, and remain, amazed that my mother was able to break out of her stupor. I've seen other people *not* make the same adjustment, at tremendous cost, but for my mom it came from being clear ultimately about what really mattered to her most, what she valued—and being humble enough (I'll say meek later on) to alter her perspective. I never heard her admit that she had been wrong because that wasn't even what it was all about. She simply saw her own **stupidity**, not in an absolute sense, but in relationship to her own life and what mattered most to her.

The challenge I see facing those of us who choose to engage completely and willfully with the outsourced economy is to get awake and to stay awake to ourselves and what matters most to us. The example of my mother is easy to understand. Day-to-day life in the workplace, on the other hand, can be far more dangerous because the opportunities to go to sleep—even after we have woken up—abound. We must be vigilant!!!

A key component of my work is in developing leaders for business who are prepared to lead in the current economic climate and deal effectively with the "outsourced abhorrent" mindset. In my firm, our belief is that the most effective leaders in the modern work environment are ones who are clear about, a) what they are about as a person, and b) the value they have to provide in the marketplace for talent. **Only people like this can be trusted to lead.** This is a strong statement, but one we think it is easy to provide evidence for. Unless a person is clear on their purpose and personal mission, they have little understanding of what their work mission might be, and probably less about their true value. A person like this can be compromised because when push comes to shove, as it often does in the workplace, they cannot be counted on to make decisions that balance the interest of the business and its stakeholders, or, more simply put, *do the right thing.*

Unfortunately, I believe this may be the case for "most people." You see, on some level these folks believe they *need* their job. They do not see themselves as solely responsible for their own economic welfare; they are dependent on the organization, not interdependent. They have no center for themselves and the things they truly care about, therefore they have no real **integrity**. I don't mean honesty here. You could leave your wallet on the desk with "most people" and leave the room without concern. What I am pointing to here is a much more profound and timeless concept. Here's one person's expression of the integrity I mean:

> *Having integrity... means being completely true to what is inside you—to what you know is right... what you feel you must do, regardless of the immediate cost or sacrifice... to be honorable and to behave decently.*
>
> Samuel Goldwyn, 1960

Now don't be picky about where you encounter the truth! "Most people" may well be very nice people, they just cannot be trusted at crunch time to do the right thing. They are dangerous to those around them and to the business they are a part of. They are much like my mother before her awakening.

In our work with business leaders we place a great deal of emphasis on the individual leader breaking the grip of any form of dependency, developing a willingness to continually monitor their relationship to their employer, advocating fearlessly for change—and if need be, to move to a different working environment if they cannot meet their personal needs in their current surroundings. At first glance it may sound like I am promoting self-centeredness...I am.

I am promoting what Charles Handy refers to as "proper selfishness" in his book, *The Hungry Spirit*:

> *What I term "proper selfishness" builds on the*
> *fact that we are inevitably intertwined with others,*
> *even if sometimes we wish we weren't, but accepts*
> *that it's proper to be concerned with ourselves and*
> *a search for who we really are, because that search*
> *should lead us to realize that self-respect, in the end,*
> *only comes from responsibility, responsibility for*
> *other people and other things.*

You might guess that at some points during our development programs people choose to leave the employer who is sponsoring our work, and you would be right! Our experience has been that somewhere around 15% of the people in our leadership programs leave the employ of the sponsor while we are working with them. The logic we offer to the sponsor, and the logic they accept, is that both parties are better off if the person leaving recognizes that there is nothing wrong with, or in, the employing company; it just isn't a fit for them. Chances are good there was something not quite right in the situation before we came along, but nobody could put their finger on it.

Much has been written already on the topic of creating a life purpose and having a personal mission statement—

by much more informed sources than myself, I would hasten to add. If you are looking for guidance in this area I would suggest one of Stephen Covey's offerings, or you might want to look at Mark Albion's book, *Making a Life... Making a Living: Reclaiming Your Purpose and Passion in Business and in Life.* I find it inspiring, readable and loaded with lots of great quotes that make the read more fun. While I think Stephen Covey's messages are timeless, I think for these days Mark Albion's approach may be more specifically timely because he is clearly all the way over to the outsourced economy mindset.

In the first chapter of *Making a Life*, Albion builds a great case for the creation of a life purpose by posing a set of questions to himself: "How could I integrate my need for spirituality and love with the desire for material comforts and the good life? How could I stop keeping score the old way and start keeping score a new way? How could I build a truly successful happy life—one of significance? How could I spend my life in a community of people whom I love and who love me in return?" I am a sucker for people who see life the same way I do. How about you? I particularly like finding really successful, well-known, former Harvard professors to quote and make my points for me.

In my view, what Mark Albion has done for us here is accurately frame the dilemma that has faced every one of us who struggle with the quandry of making a living or making a life. When the fate of our future was in the hands of someone else, as in the mindset of "most people," this is an almost impossible dilemma to solve. But what if we look with the mindset of an entrepreneur?

"I am now and forever responsible for my own financial welfare..."

This becomes a situation to be chosen, not a problem to be solved, and the circumstances are now very much in favor of choosing to satisfy both sets of priorities. Like no other time in recent history. But you have to know what you are about; you have to be responsible for getting and keeping yourself awake. Mark Albion shares the story of his personal awakening as a result of a family tragedy, as does Charles Handy in his writings. To this extent they were fortunate; something outside them knocked hard and they recognized it as opportunity.

But do you really want to trust your own awakening to a roll of the dice of life, for a personal tragedy to get your attention? Maybe not. There is the low road but there is also the high road, often less traveled. It is up to you. That's why these guys write the books, you know.

5

What's Your Deal?

Doing business as your own agent
in the Borderless World.

What do you really want in
a working environment?

Why might you settle for
something less?

C arl Jung once wrote about the cost of leading an unfulfilling life, and I'll paraphrase him here... "There is nothing so devastating to the future of a child as witnessing the unfulfilled life of a parent." I like what this suggests because it points to the notion that we do not live our lives for ourselves alone. Whatever we do or don't do affects the lives of others—that is just the way it is. From this you could infer that we have a certain responsibility to each other. I believe this; I believe it must also be true in the places we work.

This is one of the great paradoxes of life. We are put here in separate compartments and yet we are always part of something much greater than ourselves, something that we affect and something that affects us. We are educated to focus on our individual success and yet we do not achieve that success alone, despite appearances. So much attention is given to the celebration of the individual in our culture that we can and do become numb to the reality of our interdependence. There is a sadness that goes with this numbness, but it is one we don't often speak about, because we are fearful of what it means.

So why then focus any attention on ourselves, on what we want, our purpose, our mission, etc., if we are all part of this great interdependence? For the simple fact that the way through the paradox is an understanding of and responsibility for our needs. Without this understanding it is virtually impossible to appreciate and participate in the interdependence with any real power. I am convinced that those among us who are the most fun to work with, the ones who make each day worth showing up at work for, the ones from whom we learn the most, would most like to be like, and so on, are the ones who are clear about, 1) their abilities and limitations, 2) their purpose in life, 3) their personal mission, 4) their reasons for working where they do, and 5) their conditions of satisfaction. These are the folks who are leading satisfying lives; they are not necessarily the highest paid or highest placed folks in the organization, that is not necessarily their prime motivation—and you know it and you know who they are. We admire these people and yet they are often the ones we are most afraid of, because they are true to themselves, and we may well be afraid of what that means for us.

In previous chapters I talked about the value of having a clearly stated purpose for your life and a mission for yourself. Now I want to talk about perhaps the most revolutionary part of setting yourself up to be *the change you want to see happen in the workplace*. Point 5 from the paragraph above starts the conversation. Knowing what your "conditions of satisfaction" are and being uncompromising about them, is the way to becoming a card-carrying agent for yourself in any workspace. Remember this mantra: **My mother is not coming, so it must be up to me...**

to not do this alone. Let me share another story.

A client of mine, a CEO, came to me and wanted to talk about what Edwards Deming called "driving fear out of the organization." He was concerned that his industry, telecommunications, was going through a period of tremendous upheaval; competition was beginning to ramp up and he could see in his leadership team a deer-in-the-headlights tendency at the prospect of moving quickly, taking risks and all the other behaviors needed to operate successfully in the new business environment. His dilemma was whether to bring in new leadership from the outside—folks more conversant with competitive environments—or to see if it was possible to develop the necessary behaviors from among currently employed folks in leadership positions, or in the process of being groomed. I found this to be an exciting problem.

I suggested to him that if he was talking to me, he had probably already made up his mind, since he knew my bias would be to go for the option of developing the people within, but I wanted to know his thought process. Why, when it is so often the popular move to bring in "new blood," was he hesitant? Certainly the changes in the industry were interesting enough to attract very talented people. He said that he had given that a lot of thought and knew that the option was there and that my assessment of the situation was accurate. He had decided that the fresh talent outside would be his ace in the hole if the people from the inside could not step up to the challenge. He felt that it would be of greater long-term benefit to the organization if he could foster this kind of development from within, and he wanted my firm to help him craft an approach to developing a new type of leader for his company; he did not believe he could do it on his own.

At the outset I applauded his thinking. I told him my belief was that given the mindset of many in his company, outside leadership talent wouldn't have much opportunity to succeed anyway; they would be viewed as a vote of no confidence in the current leadership, and be a less-than-subtle message from senior management. The outsiders' contribution would be resisted and the investment suboptimized. However, if his folks themselves could begin to see the organization as a fluid entity with people coming and going as their talents were needed, it would then become possible to have outsiders make a contribution—but not before. I told him that making the organization a welcome space for new talents would be imperative in the long term, since the projected rapid pace of change would almost surely dictate that no organization could rely solely on its own ability to develop internal talent fast enough to keep up. The implication of what I was telling him was that some among the incumbent leadership group would have to leave, but not be let go—just given the opportunity to make a choice. And their leaving would need to be celebrated as a contribution to the whole and serve as an announcement to the entire organization that a new way of doing business was being introduced.

Here we had a company that was an icon of the old cradle-to-grave era, and here I was, advocating letting people leave graciously; and moreover, making that a popular move! If we were going to be able to introduce a new type of leadership into the organization it needed to be done without making anyone feel bad, like they had done something wrong, or they weren't good enough—because that wasn't really true, and that wasn't our intention. I told him this was not going to be an overnight project, and he allowed that he knew this and would not have trusted anything that sounded like a short-term solution.

As a first step we had to accomplish two things: The first was to clarify and communicate a new set of expectations for the behavior of anyone in a leadership role. The second was to actively de-emphasize the notions of Commitment and Loyalty to the organization (the primary promoters of fear) and to emphasize the notion of Being Effective.

At the time, I offered this scenario without having the helpful guidance of Abraham Maslow's republished work, *Maslow on Management*. I highly recommend this classic book. In the section, "Additional Notes on Self Actualization, Work, Duty and Mission," Maslow speaks directly to the point I was making: "The test for any person is—that is, what you want to find out is whether he or she is an apple tree or not—Do they bear apples? Do they bear fruit? That's the way you tell the difference between fruitfulness or sterility, between talkers or doers, between the people who change the world and the people who are helpless in it."

My client the CEO did not have the benefit of Maslow's wisdom at that point either, but he was pretty certain that he had inherited a bunch of talkers and he needed to turn them into apple trees.

Once this first step was initiated, the second action was to give people an opportunity to choose to leave with dignity. This was not one of those layoffs disguised as a generous offer from a company to retire early. This was an honest opportunity for people who had put in many years of service in a Commitment/Loyalty kind of environment, to assess the requirements of the new deal and decide whether or not to play. As you might expect, some people chose to leave and the ones who stayed knew that there was a new game afoot and they wanted to participate.

The third step in this process was to begin an active development program of leaders who would be "bulletproof." This was a term I used at the time to portray the notion that if leaders were going to be able to be counted on to "do the right thing" they must be impervious to the threat, real or imagined, of losing their job for saying the wrong thing, for making a mistake, for offering a dissenting opinion—or any other of the many things that people had come to fear as signs that they were not Loyal or Committed. Didn't it used to be that getting the label of not being "on the team" was about as bad as it could get? This idea of being bulletproof was most surely a formula for getting to eat lunch alone, at least until employees saw that doing the right thing was not just being encouraged, it was being recognized and rewarded.

As a sort of sidebar, let's admit that this sort of thing goes on everywhere. As recently as two years ago, another client heard that there was an opening in his firm for a new chief financial officer. He asked the incumbent CFO if he could be considered for the position, having had lots of financial management experience and knowing his own aspirations. He was treated with great disrespect for even making the suggestion. Couldn't he see that if he was a viable candidate he would already be under consideration? Didn't he trust the judgment of his senior management? To be honest, my client was dumbfounded. Until that moment he had never considered leaving his company of twenty years service. He was asking because he wanted to find out what deficiencies he had, if any, so he could work on them for the future. But he received no satisfaction for his attempted dialogue. Within six months this fellow had left the organization and is now CEO of a smaller firm in the same industry. In a flash of awareness he became bulletproof. This son of the Age of Willing Dependency suddenly became a citizen of the brave new world and he hasn't looked back. Almost overnight, with the unwitting assistance of the old patriarchy, he became an agent for himself in a borderless world—a free agent.

So back now to this process of becoming bulletproof. In much the same fashion as I have been taking you through the chapters of this book, we took our telecommunications client's new leadership candidates through an eight-month process of developing awareness to become leaders for the future. As I suspected and had communicated to my client, some of the participants in this program woke up in the middle and discovered that they too were not in the right place for them. They left the company, with dignity and approval. My client said he thought that if there was to be any integrity in the process, this had to happen. He saw that these people were making choices that were ultimately in the best interest of both themselves *and* the company—again, the notion of the interdependence that affects us all. He said that if these folks did not truly feel that where they were was right for them, they would reflect this feeling in their performance and it would affect those around them. This is precisely the point of becoming bulletproof.

But that's not the end of the story. Now, some seven years later, with several more of these programs complete, some of the folks who left earlier are returning. They are back not because they made a wrong decision in the first place; rather, they went out, gained some valuable experience and a big boost of self-confidence and now see more opportunity for themselves in coming back to help build the new environment. It is once again part of their future and they are welcomed back with open arms. And why not? Is it that easy to find great people who can come right into your business and be productive?

So what is your Deal? By this time I have become very clear that I do not have the time—nor is it very cost effective for every company—to have the epiphany that my CEO client friend experienced, and then offer the right type of sponsorship for his organization. Finding another paragon of enlightened management behavior would take me back to wishing mode, seeking for another Ralph Stayer or Max DuPree The changes we all want to see happen in our work places will more likely occur like cake batter being mixed, than a linear process anyway. You've seen cake batter mixed right? The ingredients are placed in the mixing bowl and then continuously folded in upon one another until everything is spread evenly throughout the batter. The ingredients do not mix themselves; they are acted upon by an external force. Left to their own devices, all these ingredients would never become a cake. In the case of my metaphor you take on the role of the outside force, but from the inside!

Well there you have it. You are not the total change that needs to happen, but you do have a choice of what role you want to play. Do you want to be a simple ingredient or the baker? However, it cannot just be me saying so. In fact my saying so has no effect whatsoever. You must choose your role, and to do so with confidence you must make that entrepreneurial declaration I have talked about, and you must also be clear what you are about and what you will take in exchange for your full participation, your conditions of satisfaction. The choice is yours: flavor or be flavored—take your pick.

As you will recall, in the Age of Willing Dependency you did not have a voice in the process of organizational development, you were an ingredient. Being happy to be mixed in or folded was your lot and grateful was the recommended state of mind. Conditions of Satisfaction were dictated by those who doled out opportunity and you sort of made the best of it. This was not a bad life; but it was an illusion, an artificial state made possible only by the flukey circumstances of the post-WWII world. As with all flukes, this one has been unmasked of course, but without an opportunity for you to vote.

It's a funny thing about people—in the wild animal kingdom when the antelope gets eaten by the lion, there is no public outcry, no headline in the paper, just an antelope carcass. And life goes on. We are not especially disturbed seeing the playing out of a natural cycle of life. But in the human world, the world of illusion, any *ripple* in the predictability of our everyday life is viewed as something gone wrong.

A possible headline in my local paper: "Today in Rochester, New York, Kodak announced that it will be cutting back employment worldwide to the tune of 10,000 employees by the end of 2006!" The subtitle might be, "2,000 of the job losses will likely affect Kodak employees in Rochester!" The response locally would be (and actually has been) that something is wrong. Nothing is wrong; this is a system making systematic adjustments. This is the illusion of security uncloaked, as Helen Keller told us it would be. We find it fascinating to watch Discovery Channel and marvel at the anxiety that must pervade the world of the antelope every day. But what about you? Considering yourself in the very same scenario as the Antelope is likely far from fascinating; it is more likely distressing. How attractive is the prospect of waking each day to immediately face the reality that your situation is something like...run or be eaten!! But that has always been your situation, it was ever thus and there was also the illusion.

That is why the concept of lifelong learning is more than just an encouragement, it is now a necessity. Staying fast as long as possible, if you are an antelope, or staying fast as long as you want to if you are a human in the workforce. Is this one of your Conditions of Satisfaction—the opportunity to continue to learn as a participant in any working environment?

So I'll ask again...what are your Conditions of Satisfaction? What are your material aspirations? How much do you need to earn to meet them? Do you know your market value? Do you understand the kinds of people you prefer to work with? Do you know the kind of work that really turns you on, makes you sing? Do you have a personal understanding of what real achievement is for you?

Let's go back to Maslow for a moment. In *Maslow on Management* he states, "What is not worth doing is not worth doing well." This is a message to each of us and also to those who employ others. Maslow is not saying that there are some tasks not worth doing. He is saying that unless we have a calling to the work, there is a high probability that it will not be done well. We don't get clear on this ourselves as we pursue a paycheck, and employers make the profound mistake of thinking that just because someone can do something, they will do it well. In the Age of Willing Dependency maybe yes, but in today's world...no!

Now recall the Maslow quote at the start of the book: *The only happy people I know are the ones who are working well at something they consider important.* He goes on to declare that he feels so strongly on this point that he considers it to be a universal truth. Note that he did not say, "working on something they considered interesting or entertaining." He said, "something they consider important." My experience in doing what I consider to be important work is that some of the time it is interesting, some of the time it is entertaining, and some of the time it is boring and difficult. When it is boring or difficult (which is after all only my opinion) is it any less important?—which is again, my opinion to begin with. Can you see how much we actually have to say about how it goes for us, but do we say it? Believe it or not—and you may not right away—what sets you up for fear in the first place is never having spoken to yourself about what it is you really want.

Before we go too far with this conversation about knowing what you want, I'd like to distance it from the romantic image on the cover of Fortune magazine a few years back, showing the young man with the parakeet on his head. Do you remember it? The quote that accompanied the picture was, "Yo Corporate America! I want a fat starting salary, a signing bonus and a cappuccino machine—oh, and I'm bringing my bird to work. I'm the new organization man. You need me." This is not, I repeat, *not* the attitude or approach I am seeking to promote.

My notion of being clear about your Deal includes

being aware of the position you are in by virtue of the circumstances. In part your value will always be determined by the circumstances, what's hot and what's not. If you want to be a true, functioning agent for yourself you must possess an awareness of the time to advance or change your skill set or your knowledge base. Before that, you must be aware that as an entrepreneurial thinker your reward will always be determined by someone else's perception of value. The interdependence thing again; there is no escaping it!

So let's finally get to the topic of knowing your Deal and being serious about it. The "how-to" of it has already been said by several folks better than I ever could. I am going to turn you over to the good guidance of Bill Bridges and Mark Albion. Mark's book, *Making a Life/ Making a Living*, has been referenced earlier and I recommend it, along with—and I mean read both authors—just about anything written by Bill Bridges. What you will not find is the formula for success; you *will* find many things to help you think this through. You will also find that Mark Albion used all the really good quotes, which is why I am using so few.

For my part, what I have to offer can be summed up by an example we use in our leadership development program. When it comes to participating in the workplace and finding a home for yourself, the situation is much like when you used to go to the high school dance. Were you there to "dance" or were you there to dance with him or her? Knowing what you are up to makes all the difference.

6

The Meek Shall Inherit the Earth

Turning a greatly misunderstood spiritual teaching
into a practical guide for maintaining
an attitude that supports adaptability

Meek: *adjective,* humbly patient

*...a new commandment has been given to us: thou
shalt love your life with all your strength and
energy, growing daily in appreciation of the joys of
life; and you shall allow and aid where possible your
neighbor to love his and do the same, using common
norms of justice to determine life's priorities. Live to
make life livable: fighting when necessary, learning
by whatever means possible, having a good time
when you feel like it, respecting life's mysteries in
an active, not a passive manner. In short, love life
—and do whatever you want.*
Matthew Fox, *On Becoming a Musical Mystical Bear*

These opening words come from a man who did not
just say them, he also lived them. Matthew Fox, a former Dominican monk considered by the Catholic Church

to be a spiritual maverick, is the author of over twenty books on spirituality. His insistence on asking and promoting dialogue around tough spiritual questions eventually led to his expulsion by Church leadership after twenty-seven years in his order. Perhaps taken at face value, these words of Fox's might be interpreted as inflammatory, dangerous to a societal approach to living. Often, when I quote Fox in any discussion of self-expression in the workplace, someone will ask if I am promoting anarchy. Fox's critics accused him of something similar, but in his case he was being accused of undermining the spiritual absoluteness of the leadership of his church. From my considerable reading of his work I would say that nothing could be further from the truth. If anything, he offers pathways for thinking that would deepen faith and diminish the weight given to simply following rules—as though that were a measure of the health of one's spiritual life.

His words encourage us to realize a greater sense of responsibility for our own lives. I believe he is encouraging us to be bold and courageous—the same kind of boldness that Helen Keller was speaking to in the Preface to this book. Fox exhorts us to make our life a learning experience from beginning to end, to meet life on its own terms and adopt a student's mind in doing so. Let life teach us. This does not sound like the American Way. Neither Fox nor Keller would have us view life as a contest—"The one who dies with the most toys wins!" As I understand life, if the slogan were to say, "The one who dies with the most toys still dies!" it might encourage us to pursue the theme of this chapter, a learning and experiential approach to our lives. But the word "meek" in the chapter heading does present a challenge. What could *meek* possibly have to do with being bold and courageous?

I have wrestled with writing this chapter ever since I had the idea that I wanted to put something in this book about how to "be" in this new economic world. Even using the term how to "be" may make me suspect here, but I am literally referring to the way we meet the world, the window of our own experience. I'm here to tell you, this is the stuff reality is made of. In the preface of one of his most recently published books, *Waiting for the Mountain to Move*, Charles Handy speaks to the struggle I am attempting to illuminate:

> *The search for that connection between belief and action (my being and my doing) is never-ending and always changing because the world and its problems is always changing. The beliefs may remain the same, but their applications will always need to be rethought by each of us each year, even each day. We are forever going to be searchers after the truth.*

And I would add, "...or we are not!" Perhaps this is the likeliest of outcomes. I do not mean to sound cynical in this instance, for I am not.

The notion of personal transformation is not new, particularly in this era in America. Books, tapes and programs abound, intended to give us greater access to peace of mind as a result of seeing the world in a new light. As far as I can tell, the motivation for this kind of searching comes from an individual's sensing that "something is just not right." I think what they sense is that there is a gap between their "being" and their "doing," and it is causing them discomfort. Some methods are ancient (meditation, yoga and martial arts come to mind) and some are more modern in their origin. No matter the source, there is plenty of evidence that many folks in today's world are not getting everything they need, either in life or in the workplace, and they are beginning to suspect that maybe this has something to do with *them*, not their circumstances. I happen to think that anyone looking for peace of mind, personal transformation or an attitude overhaul might as well embrace the workplace as they search for their own truth, for the obvious reason that we spend so much of our life there.

I have actually heard people say that the way they are at work is "not really the way they are." I cannot think of a sadder declaration about the conditions of one's life than that. Just a moment of thought would put that statement in the category of someone receiving a life sentence for suffering. Like saying, "Well, let's see, I have 100% of my life to live, take away 35-40 years when I'll need to be somebody else except for the weekends. OK, I'll make that deal...but you won't bother me on the weekends, right?"

The silliness that we labor with throughout our life is the notion that the only way we could be truly free, happy —whatever you want to call it—is if we had complete control of everything we do. The truth is we do. Even in an alley with a mugger pointing a gun to our head, we have complete control of ourselves. Yes, but we have no control over the circumstances, you say. And my response would be, "Ever it were thus." We have never had control of the circumstances. We have only had the illusion of control, a mental trick we play to convince ourselves that we are more powerful than the circumstances of life. We are in control, we convince ourselves, therefore we are safe.

Ah, you say, but wait, let's get back to that mugger thing you were talking about; there is no illusion of control there. And I say, Thank goodness you noticed. You are in the presence of the daring adventure. Your awareness of the danger makes you less likely to do something to make matters worse. The problem in the alley is no different from the problem we face when we make the statement, "I have to go to work today." No you don't. You don't have to go to work. You don't have to work where you do. You don't have to do what a boss tells you. You don't have to work for what you are being paid. You don't have to do anything!!! (And please try to believe me, I'm still not advocating for anarchy.)

The problem, the real problem, is that most of us don't like what this means—that we don't *have* to do anything. The real problem is not that we don't have the freedom; it's that we have more than we want to be responsible for. What I believe is really going on most of the time is that we are confusing the concept of freedom with the desire for control. The hard reality of life is that we have virtually no control over the circumstances and complete freedom in our response to the circumstances. Once you get cleared up on the confusion about where you do and do not have control—between the circumstances and you—the mysterious nature of satisfaction begins to unravel.

As I am writing I can hear the arguments beginning to line up. What about this awful situation and what about that situation; people living under oppressive governments, the unjustly imprisoned? Certainly not fair, I agree, and neither is the fact that my neighbor down the street wins the New York State Lottery and I don't. It is the same. In the alley, we have the freedom to say no to the mugger and take our chances. I can also play the lottery and take my chances. That is the kind of choice this chapter is *not* about; I am not talking about options. Options involve selecting from among a variety of possible responses. Whereas, *choosing* means to see the circumstances for what they are and accept them without judgment. In doing so we create the condition required for freedom.

Seeing and accepting things as they are, or pretty close to the way they are, allows us to act freely. The act is chosen, not forced by any circumstance. At the end of my alley scenario the odds are you will end up without your wallet. However, there will be a big difference between how you are left from the experience: no wallet, victimized, violated and made less powerful, or no wallet, not victimized and relieved for having survived the encounter, ready to get on with your life.

The issue is not one of freedom, it is one of not being really clear about what matters most to us, and then being serious about it: What do we have control over and what do we not; and whether we are prepared to deal with the consequences of our actions with responsibility. And finally, of course, understanding the risk/reward scenario. I am not going to address the issue of consequences. That you can deal with on your own. You are there in the alley, you have a choice, give up your wallet or not. In this chapter I am more interested in how you "be," and less interested in which choice you ultimately make. This is where being really clear about your life purpose and mission comes into play. If you know that you have places to go and things to do when that mugger pops up in the alley, you most likely turn over your wallet, thank him for not shooting or stabbing you and get on with your life ... but really get on with your life, not like a victim who got robbed in an alley and it shouldn't have happened blah, blah, blah. You can either be grateful or victimized. Where do you think there is more life?

If the "you" that's in that alley is not clear what you are all about, you might just get indignant or worse, think it was time someone showed this mugger a thing or two. Yes, you would be right. This person should not be taking your wallet. There is also something else you might be: dead right. Sort of says it all in this instance.

Now, what about the term *meek* in the title of this chapter? I have been talking about it for several paragraphs without saying the word. Back in the alley when you recognized that you had places to go and things to do and you gave over your wallet to the mugger...that was meekness, not weakness.

Along about 1934, a New Thought lecturer named Emmet Fox (no relation to Matthew) wrote a book called, *The Sermon on the Mount: The Keys to Success in Life*. In this relatively thin volume he speaks in depth about the application of the Sermon's teachings. Regarding the declaration by Jesus, "Blessed are the meek, for they shall inherit the earth," Fox states his belief that this is among the most misunderstood verses in the entire Bible; and yet he considers it to be among the half-dozen most important. Fox writes that there are two points of misinterpretation, one being the understanding of the word "meek" and the other of the word "earth."

Earlier, I said that we have far more control over our lives than we care to be responsible for. In this interpretation of the teachings of Christ, Fox is suggesting pretty much the same thing. Fox sees the term meek as having little to do with the modern usage of the word—submissive, weak, without will, behaviors that are far from powerful or attractive. He says that Christ was using the term in a very technical sense, referring to a mental attitude "for which there is no other single word available." A closer meaning for the meek of the Sermon might be: flexible, receptive, humble. Fox states, "When you possess the spiritual meaning of this text you have the secret of dominion—the secret of overcoming every kind of difficulty. It is literally the key to life." How about that for a bold statement? By the way, Fox's writings—and there were many—have long been a mainstay of the Alcoholics Anonymous philosophy.

At first glance we may think Fox is saying that somehow by following this teaching we can gain control. Sorry, no such luck! He goes on to talk about the other troublesome word in the verse, "earth," which in his opinion is Christ referring to the ability we all have to create our experience of life. The earth might also be called the world, and perhaps it is easier if we think in terms of control over our world (experience) than the earth; at least it is for me. So, he says, if we are meek (teachable, coachable, the Buddhists call it beginner's mind) things can go pretty well for us. My reference here is from the teachings of Christianity, but any examination of another fully developed spiritual cosmology would show this to be a pretty universal principle.

How does this relate to thriving in a changing world? One who would fully engage with the outsourced economy would do well to develop the practice of meekness as a foundation for adaptability. Emmet Fox refers us to the image of Moses as an example of this trait in practice, reminding us that while he had his flaws, throughout his life he was open to being taught new ways of thinking and working. Moses so embodied this principle of meekness that it even affected his physical appearance; he was said to have maintained a youthful countenance even at a very advanced age. As far as I know, we have no pictures of Moses to verify the fact of his youthfulness, but how many of you have people in your lives who at an advanced age are still young, at least in spirit. I'm willing to bet that this can at least partly be attributed to what Fox is calling meekness. I am often struck by meeting folks who appear and act considerably older than I am, only to find that they in fact are younger! How do I explain the difference? I can't in any scientific way, but I do know that I remain very curious, have re-thought my world view several times with the help of many friends, and do my best to stay open to new ideas. Even though my own practice is far from rigorous, I can vouch for the notion that this manner of staying young is available to anyone. It may boil down to something as simple as waking each morning with a sense that you still have places to go and things to do and you are grateful for the opportunity to have a future.

The Practice of Gratitude

I am going to recommend the Practice of Gratitude as the primary method for remaining meek, all other disciplines notwithstanding. We've all heard the phrase, "Hey, you deserve it, you work hard." It is symbolic shorthand from the era in which we exchanged the time of our lives for a paycheck, and the illusion of security—a period whose shadow still has many in darkness. Where did we ever get the idea that just because we work hard we deserve anything? From the same period that brought us the notion that businesses were benevolent institutions that could provide or guarantee lifetime employment.

In many people's experience the single most missing element in their day-to-day work lives is **appreciation**, the experience of receiving the report of someone else's gratitude for services rendered. I am not talking about recognition, like the awkward and non-spontaneous Employee Recognition Programs found in many businesses. These can be just one more reason to not express appreciation. I'm not damning Employee Recognition, but if these programs are played out in an environment that lacks fundamental appreciation, they are hollow and inauthentic.

I recall a woman who worked for my company in a temporary assignment a couple of years ago. She was doing a lot of administrative work for me and on one occasion she came to me and asked a question that I found amazing. "Why do you always say 'Thank you' when I turn over something I have finished for you?" The question took me back for a moment and then I asked her if it was unusual in her experience for her to be thanked. She said, "Well, yes, and besides, I am just doing my job."

The way I see it, whatever one person does for another in the workplace, it usually takes a certain investment to deliver, a balancing of priorities, some thought, and an intention to meet someone else's needs. This means that performance is never guaranteed and the "thank you" is my way of recognizing my appreciation for the support, and also that it took something from the person to deliver what I needed. I just never take it for granted that people are going to be able to manage all the variables in order to do what is needed. Beyond that, this practice also contributes to maintaining a healthy humility. I constantly remind myself through the practice of saying "thank you" that I do not deserve people's support; it is their gift to me. That they get paid is immaterial to the notion of being grateful. It also serves as a constant reminder that whatever I am doing or trying to accomplish, I am not doing it alone.

"I am not doing this alone, I am not doing this alone, I am not doing this alone...and the people who support me value and benefit from my appreciation."

This could be your mantra, or you could make up your own. The point would be to do something to remind yourself to thank people, thank people, and thank people as a practice that will make your world a more satisfying place to live in.

7

Being Engaged Means Being Related

If you are conscious there is no other
conclusion. Being able to get related is
the foundation of adaptability

No man is an island, entire of itself; every man is a
piece of the continent.

John Donne, *Meditation XVII*

I f John Donne were alive today he might amend his quote
here to say "...every man is a piece of the world." Very
likely neither Donne nor his contemporaries in the late
1500's could have imagined a world anything like the one
we have created for ourselves. In this world, states, nations,
even continents have lost the historical meanings of separation. Geographic distance means very little unless you
are considering vacation travel. In order to do business in
any part of the world you do not even need to leave your
computer keyboard. But you do need to know how to get
connected and develop knowledge of staying connected.

Consider this statement a moment: *"The nature of*
exchanges... have therefore become the medium through which

value is delivered." In other words, the true value in our lives will be measured by how we are related to or engaged with those people who can act as resources for us—and we for them. The quote is from *Blur,* by Stan Davis and Chris Meyer; more from them later.

What would it take for you to fully accept the implication of this? What would it mean to your sense of Self and island-ness? Can you see that acceptance of interdependence will evoke humility from each of us or we will not survive, much less thrive?

If you are going to be able to turn this book into anything of value for yourself (and why else read it?) this is the point of no return. From here on in you will either engage with what I'm suggesting, or you don't. This is the point where we connect, if we have not already. You will be up for trying my recommendations, or something close to them (your way of course!)—or you won't. You'll know by the time you are done reading this chapter. If you decide not to proceed, then give the book to someone you know who shares your concerns for their economic viability in the future. Keep tabs on whether they finish the book. If they do, definitely stay in touch with them because I'm pretty sure you will want the book back in a short while. Remember, just because you don't believe something or it makes you uncomfortable, doesn't mean it's without value to your life. That's OK. I am a school of hard knocks guy myself.

Pay Attention: A Controlled Experiment
I am going to ask you to do a little experiment. Nothing too demanding, but it can tell you a lot. For a week, if you can, or at least a couple of days, keep track of all the connections you have with people in your workplace who have something to do with your work getting done. No essays here, just notes to yourself.

Here's what to keep track of:

1) What do you expect to be getting from another person that is supposed to add value to your process? Was it on time? Was it what you really needed? Was it completely usable when you received it?

2) What are you supposed to be delivering to other people? Are you clear from your customer interactions, internal or external, when something is needed and what it really needs to be?

After making these observations for a while, you will start to get the point of the experiment. Your getting your work done has everything to do with how you and the other people are related, not whether they like you or even know you, in the sense of being familiar with you personally. The relationship, the connection, will ultimately determine the quality of the results you can come to expect, or that others can expect from you. This can be a tough inquiry because you will very likely get to see yourself "prioritize" what you have told others you would deliver, as you attempt to balance the complexity of commitments you have made at any point in time, including those to your family and even to yourself. Each prioritized commitment carries with it the possibility of being "morphed" into a good story rather than a satisfied customer when time and the work to be done collide, and someone must be disappointed.

The Nature of Engagement

When I start talking about being engaged in the workplace I am talking about what there is "to do." More importantly, I am also talking about "being," and most specifically being engaged with life, being connected to life, because it is all the same. I see the workplace as a metaphor, a model, for life. For about nineteen years now I have been working with folks in the workplace on the art of being engaged and the skills of being related. Almost always the conversation begins by my letting people know that they will have to give up what they already mean by "related."

To begin with, I am not talking about "Do you know someone," as the basis for being related. That's most people's place to start, not mine. I am talking about relationships you generate from your own engagement with what you're trying to get done in your lifetime. I am defining something much more profound than simply knowing someone. I am talking about the practice or discipline of being engaged. This is much different from, say, "how to feel at ease at parties." Generating relationships is a practice and a discipline; it takes work and breaking out of self-imposed limits. It is not just something that sort of happens randomly in the course of your life. Let's go back to a definition I used in the Introduction:

Engage: *verb,* to choose to involve oneself in or commit oneself to something, as opposed to remaining aloof or indifferent

To engage, then, is to take the circumstances as they are, without reservation. Now, choosing to actively participate with "the way it is" without needing to have a say or a vote may not seem at first glance to be powerful, yet I believe it is. This is much more than making lemonade out of lemons. The kind of engagement perspective I am promoting might go like this: "OK, I see how it is, I accept how it is. Now what do I want and how do I leverage the way that it is to accomplish my vision?" There is no adaptation required of me at this point; rather, I have just made a declaration of power in harmony with the circumstances. I have not yet engaged myself. This will require what I am referring to as a practice or a disciplined approach.

As with any discipline or practice, I believe there are

principles and skills to be mastered in developing the confidence to effectively engage the world around us—paying attention to the nature of the exchanges we require, in order to determine whether they hold the likelihood of delivering what is needed when it is needed. In my work with people in organizations I often invoke the image of a circus trapeze performance in all its cooperative, interactive dynamics. I ask whether they have ever considered the possibility of crafting working relationships to have the reliability of those effortless-looking exchanges high above the circus floor. The answer is almost always "no," but then people do admit that while they yearn for that kind of reliability they most often *plan* for some other less satisfying outcome—not realizing that contingency or "do it yourself" plans may in and of themselves undermine the opportunity for the interdependence on which organization design was premised. Quite simply, "most people" do not see the possibility. Why? Because it is not visible if you operate from the perspective of independently getting what you need. It only becomes visible when you engage the "field" of interdependence that surrounds us at all times in our lives.

Before I get too far into this I need to tell you that I have no data for what comes next, simply my observations from my years as a consultant and the years before that as an employee in an organization probably much like yours. So, what I am offering is an opinion largely informed by my own experience. Since I am not innately gifted in the arena of being related, it has been a learned practice. I came to it through engagement with my own personal vision for what I am committed to accomplishing in my lifetime.

Being able to generate the connections needed is sourced in engagement. It is fundamental to developing adaptability. To put the concept into a simple, graphic expression, I offer my basic recipe for adaptability:

Personal Responsibility + Personal Vision + Technical Competence + Collaborative Competence + Reputation = Your Adaptability Index

I am not interested in what a measure of adaptability might look like as a number. I am sharing with you what I believe must be accepted and attended to in order to develop an adaptability IQ. Of the five elements of the Adaptability Index, I am going to pay special attention to the one that has been overlooked by our education systems and misunderstood or poo-poo'd by business leaders for years: Collaborative Competence.

In any field of endeavor there are some people who are more successful than others. Do you attribute that to some people being smarter than the rest of us; more committed than the rest of us; luckier than the rest of us? Here is what I think is behind that success. For the moment we'll take Personal Responsibility and Personal Vision as givens; otherwise we are just leaving success up to luck or an accident of birth or something else we have no control over. There is no question that a person needs a certain amount of knowledge, Technical Competence, to be successful at any endeavor. On the whole I believe this factor is overrated and I invite you to check this against your own experience. We all know some pretty smart people who are only moderately successful and many are not what you'd call adaptable; some of them are pretty bitter too. We also know some pretty well educated folks in the same situation.

So now, with Personal Responsibility and Vision as givens and Technical Competence put in perspective, I'm left with Collaborative Competence (the ability to connect) and Reputation. In the working world Reputation does matter, insofar as it plays a role in determining opportunities you may be considered for or be offered. In my formula it is in fact a dependent variable. I do see Reputation as the product of Technical Competence and Collaborative

Competence; however, I add it into the formula because it is to a certain degree within your control and therefore something to be attended to. I will return later to spend more time on Reputation as it is connected to Power and Responsibility.

For now I want to stay focused on Collaborative Competence. We all have the ability to engage in developing our Collaborative Competence—how else do marriages work, when they do? What we don't do is use these tools enough in other venues to understand their power to create other valuable types of connections. There is little around us that encourages the use of Collaborative Competence as a major element of a satisfying life journey. In fact, for most of our formative lives we get very mixed messages on this topic.

We live in a culture that cares far less about being connected and "other-focused" than it does about having the things that make you think you are a success. You can get everything you want to and it does not necessarily have anything to do with satisfaction with our lives. I am sure this is not the first time you've heard this, so why do we keep going back to what we cannot get enough of to bring us the satisfaction we seek? First, *having* is much easier to grasp than *being*. Second, most of us do not know ourselves well enough to know why we would or should want to "be connected." Finally, and probably most importantly, nobody has figured out how to make money by selling *being*. When they do it will be great, as I imagine the margins are terrific.

Here is where I think the whole American Dream paradigm breaks down. It begins and ends with a lie, and the lie is in the focus on being what you want by having what you need to have. "If you have these shoes you will be a great basketball player." "Wear this deodorant and have women (men) fall at your feet!" "Drive this car and be the envy of your neighborhood, or at least the kids in the neighborhood!" As best I can tell, your "having" has little to do with your "being." Actually you "be" very little by yourself, even with the shoes, the deodorant and the car, except looking like you do. The kids call this posing. A poser is someone who has all the trappings and not necessarily the abilities associated with those same trappings. Maybe many of us are posers. Maybe we really prefer posing to being.

Being is a function of engagement, not a function of having. I am a basketball player not because I have the shoes but because I engage with the game. Nor do outcomes determine being. I am a basketball player because I engage with the game. Success is relative and is a measure of proficiency in the circumstances, not a measure of being. My proficiency at basketball makes possible playing at various levels of the game.

The essence of being is to engage with the world, and that begins with creating your own vision for your life—let's call it your dharma, that inner reference point that keeps you true to yourself. After that, almost everything else depends on your willingness to be responsible for your vision and your ability to engage with the world around you (people) in accomplishing what you have envisioned. I can play basketball anywhere I can find a level of play that matches my proficiency.

But creating a vision for yourself is no small matter. Lots of people have a clear "wish" about how they want their lives to be and how they want to live. Yet, "most people" are not prepared for the level of personal responsibility called for to transform that wish into a vision, a guiding path for their lives. The wishers play lotteries, the responsible engage with the world around them. And there are many positions along the spectrum, from wishers to responsible.

Never has a people focused as much on *having* as we have here in America during the past century. At the same time, never has a people had more opportunity to "be connected" as their chosen condition. In this moment of our history we, individually, have never been better positioned to connect with the world around us—and this potential will only increase. The available technology to facilitate connectivity clearly favors individuals over organizations, as we have known them. To many of us this change is very distressing; this is just one more move in the breakdown of familiar support structures. Some people express a growing sense of isolation rather than connection. How can this be, with all our communication technology? Maybe because "being connected" is not the same thing as "having technology." Connection is certainly an outcome of the technology available, but then again we always have a choice in how we use any tool. In effect, the connectivity being made available in the information age is only making more obvious, and in some cases more painfully obvious, the interdependence that we must embrace in order to fully participate in an outsourced, borderless economy.

Those who would succeed in this new world must be able to tolerate the paradox of *chosen individual responsibility* and *appreciated interdependence*. This is a recipe for freedom; it is not necessarily a comfortable place but it is powerful one. The need for security will be replaced by confidence. Confidence will come from being clear about what we have chosen to engage with, being prepared to never stop learning, and knowing the skills it will take to become and remain connected to the resources that you need.

Again, my recipe for adaptability:

Personal Responsibility + Personal Vision + Technical Competence + Collaborative Competence + Reputation = Your Adaptability Index

Let's take this quote from Stan Davis and Chris Meyer in their 1999 look into the future, *Blur*:

Economists have only spoken of land, labor and capital as the inputs to an economy. Although land is losing some of its relevance, otherwise it is not changing much. Labor and capital, on the other hand are changing beyond recognition. Labor is no longer thought of as hours of undifferentiated wrench-turning, but as talent, not so much to be hired as to be applied to the issue of the moment... Our discussion of people focuses on the nature of the exchanges in which this talent will be the most valued resource...

The "nature of the exchanges" these guys are talking about is what I am referring to as the quality of the relationships you craft. Building your capability for crafting and managing these exchanges will be your greatest source of confidence. It is what will make you bulletproof. Being able to unplug, reprogram, move on and plug back in is the fundamental ability that will get you through the night.

Some of us have an ability to be related naturally, but do we have the wisdom to direct the ability in what Stephen Covey calls a win-win fashion? I am going to say this here and note that it is another of my strong opinions: **I believe the true measure of the strength of any of your working relationships is whether a person is looking forward to the next transaction they complete with you.** In other words, was this exchange valuable? Were all parties satisfied or did someone come out feeling they got short-changed? Some people, and you know who they are, always seem to make things harder than they need to be. You can get what you want from them but always think twice before asking. Given the choice, you'll work around them because it's just not worth it and you never leave them feeling like you've gotten satisfaction.

Some of us learned our ability to be successfully related in a particular environment. Do we also have the wisdom and awareness to be able to apply this ability at will in another environment? The vast majority of us simply have not been prepared. We did all the right things or most of them, we thought, and what did it get us? The right to risk it all in the outsourced economy.

While I can state for a fact that there is much more individual freedom in the outsourced economy, there is also more responsibility and a very thin instruction manual. Notice I did not say there is now more risk? I don't think there is. I believe that all previous conditions of security were illusionary, and finally—in your new position of individual responsibility and appreciated interdependence—you can look forward to being in touch with the inherent risk of being alive. The notion of "jobs" in the new economy may be shifting considerably, but I think you will find that the practice of being related is a full time job, and it will never be outsourced to another location.

8

The Practice of Designing Relationships

There is a conscious approach to be learned,
and a craft to be developed, in mastering
the practice of Designing Relationships

So, are you related or not? Is that even a valid question? Are relationships like bits and bytes, either on or off? A quick assessment of your life will probably reveal that there are gradients in relationships. Sometimes I have misread where I was on the relationship gradient with a given person. Maybe I have a great co-worker and it's very satisfying working with him or her, and so I assume I'd get as much satisfaction from having a beer with them. I make the invitation for something social and find that they feel our working relationship is great and it is derived from the shared context of being at work—but they have no desire to have it be otherwise. Pardon me!

Something like this has happened to all of us I imagine, either professionally or socially. Relationships are context-bound. If you presume to place the same expectations on the relationship elsewhere as you do in the shared context, you may quickly find the limits.

But I am getting ahead of myself. Is there a gradient in relationships? I think so. The gradient is the measure of power available to realize the purpose of the relationship in the context in which it was formed. What I am talking about is displayed in this diagram.

Power as a Function of Engagement

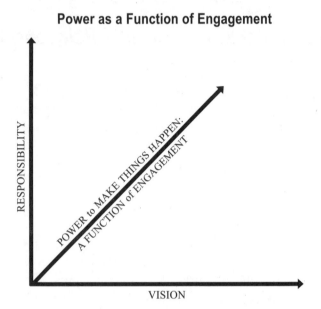

In this diagram we see what arises from the combined effects of **Responsibility** and **Vision**. Here, Responsibility has more than one meaning; it is simultaneously the ability to respond and the willingness to answer for. Vision is used here as the ability to perceive mental images, to conceptualize. Each of these is something we all can have or do. Yet, we may have vision without responsibility and be thought of as wishful thinkers, dreamers. Or we could have responsibility without vision, which may make us simply a "good person." Unfortunately, as a matter of economics in the world we live in, being a "good person" is not a complete foundation for thriving.

But Responsibility <u>with</u> Vision offers an experiential definition of Engagement – with their product being **Power**. Power can be defined in many ways. For me, it is the ability to get things done. And that is what we will look at next.

For any position on the gradient of power I believe there are distinguishable levels of engagement, but for the most part we are unaware of the distinctions in any way that makes them useful. If I ask you if you could borrow money from certain people in your life you would probably say, "Sure." If I asked if you could borrow money from *everyone* in your life you would say, "Of course not!" If I asked, among those you could borrow from, could you borrow the same amount from all of them (aside from their ability to lend)? You would undoubtedly say, "No!"

You could probably borrow cab fare from some people you know without a problem, but beyond that you are not sufficiently related. We do know these things about our relationships. However, if I asked you (and I'm not going to) if you could take one of the cab fare relationships and turn it into a $5,000 six month loan relationship (again, assuming ability to pay), would you know what to do? Hmm, what would you do? The challenge of the outsourced economy is no less daunting than that; and for those of us without the willingness or ability to generate relationships, our response can look like "falling with style," as Woody said to Buzz Lightyear in Toy Story, when commenting on his flying ability. In case you don't recall I believe the exact quote was, "Hey! That's not flying, it's falling with style." But I know you knew that.

We intuitively know that there are levels of being engaged with the people around us, whether at home or at work, but we do not necessarily know much about *designing* relationships to operate at the levels we really need them to be. We sort of either have the relationships we need or we don't. If we have them we use them to our advantage. If we don't, we often concoct some story about how some people are luckier than others; maybe it's not going to work out for us this time around, etc. Whatever the story is, it comes down to your being some kind of victim in this big game of chance called life. The victim perspective is a very complex subject area and I am going to save it for another chapter, except to comment that this is a fundamental point of differentiation between the perspective of those who will be successful in the new economy and those who will not. It goes something like this for those who get the game now:

I will thrive to the extent that I understand and apply the rules of engagement in the world today.

I recognize that my intent to deliver value to others is the entry point to engaging effectively with those who are resources to me.

I will expect no return to me until I have delivered value to another.

The bound-to-not-be-successful might verbalize this alternate perspective:

Opportunity is something that I am offered or not.

Hopefully I will be home if it ever knocks at my door.

In the meantime I will work really hard.

Maybe this sounds silly to you, and you can't imagine anyone really saying something like this to themselves, particularly the latter statement. Yet, some version of these statements—even if it remains only a thought—is fundamental to the perspective from which each of us engages the world. I am just asking you to check and see if your point of view isn't pretty close to one of these. And if you can see where I'm going with this, can you also see how your point of view affects your actions?

Now back to the notion of engagement and there being an approach to designing relationships. In the post WWII economy, when "most people" migrated towards jobs, the first level of being related might have been referred to as Satisfying Personal Economic Needs. This level was pretty much satisfied when we secured a job and it might have come as a result of the type of relationship where my abilities and my "I need a job" met up with an opening for "someone who can do this job." My need was satisfied by fulfilling a need. There wasn't much negotiation, if any. Since I was in need I took what was offered. Since the other was in need I offered only what was asked for, and nothing more. There was never any discussion of my value, i.e., what I could provide if given license to do more. Once the position was secured I could, in many cases, maintain the relationship for many years, again without negotiation, and make a living out of the fruits of my labor as they were doled out to me over time. The biggest risk I faced in this economy was the next level of being engaged, Getting Along. Since I had virtually no say about who my co-workers or supervisors were, nor they any about me, the luck of the gods of economics came into play. If I was fortunate, I rolled co-workers I could get along with and drew a supervisor who at least liked me. If not, woe unto me because "I need this job."

Probably most of us have wound up in circumstances somewhere in between. There were enough people we got along with for us to get our work done. And while we may have not been the favorite son or daughter of our manager or supervisor, they had enough of a sense of fair play that we got a bump in our favor every now and again. I know all this sounds pretty dismal and, you might even argue, not very precise, but I am giving extremes here and we all know there are degrees of everything. Well, you say, "what about those fast track people? They didn't fit this picture." Oh really! The fast trackers more proved the point than countered it, and remember their lifestyles: moving every two or three years, kids in and out of schools. Can't turn down a move, it will kill your career. It was all just a different version of the same game. Yes, it had greater rewards; it was also more painful. I think that's why we have encountered so many cynical executives over the years. They sucked it up. Why shouldn't we?

But, not to worry, because things have changed. Not only has the game changed but the skills needed to be related in life have now become the skills to be related in the workplace, so you can get a double dip! However, like many other things, being related has become more freeing and more complex, all at the same time. Relating and the ability to relate are now equal in value to what you know or can do. In many instances, being related will be even more important than what you know.

Peter Drucker has mused that we will likely not see this fundamental truth until the light of "choice" in our lives makes it visible.

Other people do not limit the choices available to us; other people are involved in the choices we make as a natural consequence.

MFC 4/6/06

If this new age is truly the Age of Choice, then it is now our destiny, I believe, to discover just how much choice we really have. If we take on this learning curve we will run smack into another fundamental truth: As human beings living in societies bounded by law, we are truly interdependent. To the degree we can willingly choose to appreciate the interdependence we might leverage this truth.

One opportunity we have in our immediate futures is to use our places of work as our classroom. Other people do not limit the choices available to us, other people are involved in the choices we make as a natural consequence.

Design for Engagement: Levels of Engagement to be addressed

Another story: One evening I was trying to answer the question, "Why don't people who are obviously able, do what they have said they will do?" This is a pretty basic question, yet one I've noticed "most people" do not consider deeply. If they don't get what they have been promised from someone they: 1) stop counting on that person, 2) ascribe the occurrence to a character defect, or 3) use the outcome to reinforce the handy belief that if you want something done right you do it yourself.

On my way to creating an answer to this question for myself I started with what may seem to be a naïve assumption: *When people say they are going to do something for you, in the moment of saying this they truly mean to do it.* No one ever accused me of being anything but naïve, so why would this be different? To conserve the resource budget I used as my control subject myself. This was then a pretty inexpensive set-up. I next asked myself what was the source of my not doing what I promised to do. I assumed here that I possessed the ability to deliver what I had promised.

What follows is an outline and brief description of what I came to understand. I started out with the premise that when I did not do as I had said I would, it involved some sort of character issue. And I was surprised to discover that something else was more likely true.

My first breakthrough came to me immediately after I released the belief that broken promises were somehow a character issue. In that new light I saw that my failures to perform were often rooted in something that was *missing*, not something that was wrong. As I settled into the inquiry I saw that in many instances I did not treat my relationships as precious; I often treated them as givens, as taken for granted. In the context of "taken for granted" we assume there will also always be understanding, there will be forgiveness. There might be consequences, but certainly nothing really final. After all, I meant well, even though I did not deliver. That had to count for something, right?

What was missing, then, was masked over by what was assumed—that being that sincerity has value, and good intentions should carry much the same weight as good results. If this sounds familiar it should. This is the theme song of a large percentage of our population who believe working hard renders you deserving of reward. This is a carryover notion from the now-bygone era when employers paid mainly for your time, not your performance. These same people believe that jobs in this country should be both created and protected by our government.

When I let go of any notions of "deserving" and replaced them with "responsibility," it became apparent that many of my working relationships were ripe for disappointment, since they had never really been designed; they had either been inherited from previous situations or conceived in a swamp of mutual assumption. As I sat at my desk that evening I simply asked myself over and over that question, "Why don't people who are obviously able, do what they have said they will do? What was missing?"

The following set of distinct levels to be addressed while Designing for Engagement rolled out of the fog of my consciousness. I did the inquiry backwards from the failed promise, tracking it to its logical source. I began to see it in terms of levels, five of them. I'll present them with the caution that relationships really cannot be broken apart as neatly as I am describing.

Here are the Big Five in a nutshell, just so you'll know where we're headed for the next few chapters. As a visual concept it looks like a set of steps or levels, with each adding to the Power to Make Things Happen.

Design for Engagement ™

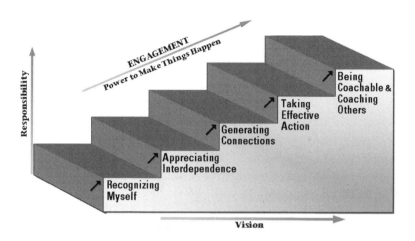

I'm going to devote a short chapter to each of the levels in the Design for Engagement, but a summary of my model is a useful place to start.

Level 1: Recognizing Myself
- Creating My Life Purpose (What am I about?)
- Creating My Life Work and Work Mission (What is my vision?)
- Understanding What Matters to Me (What's my economic Deal?)
- Knowing My Motivators (What is automatically important to me?)
- Understanding My Style (How do I go about getting things done?)
- Knowing My Natural Work (What is the sound of my song?)

Level 2: Appreciating Interdependence
The second level is characterized by two-way relating—you and others—but we'll focus on your part.

- Realizing that "independence" is an illusion.
- Recognizing and legitimizing differences in styles, values, and competencies.
- Intentionally meeting the needs of others.
- Accepting "interdependence" as the state of being for everything in our world.

If you can manage these first two levels you may begin to "see" the next level in any given relationship. You may find yourself asking if something more might be available. Could I make something out of this relationship if I made more of an investment? Thus the third level begins to emerge because people want to create something together. You begin to employ the power of commitment as something mutual, something generative, and you are now moving from being circumstantially related to being related on or with *purpose*.

Level 3: Generating Connection
- Sharing visions of a desired future in which we all win.
- Leveraging differences.
- Developing an authentic desire to know and appreciate the perspective of others.

When you move to this level of designing relationships you have crossed a threshold, and you now have the power to add value *inside* of already valuable relationships, as well as create value-adding relationships.

The fourth level to be addressed is almost obvious but tricky nonetheless. Once you have "generated" a relationship you will undoubtedly desire to see if you can make something happen. Something happening comes as an outcome of Taking Effective Action. This level, like the others, has its own set of tools, some that will seem pretty familiar and some maybe not.

Level 4: Taking Effective Action

To make something happen together we must: 1) say we are going to do certain things by certain times and mean it, and 2) ask for certain things by certain times and mean it. But how about the question of whether we can do it? Do we have the requisite knowledge, skills, resources, etc? Is this obvious? Do you always do what you say; do others always do for you what they say? The tricky part comes in when we, either you or I, have said we are going to make something happen and we are not doing what we said we were going to do, or not asking for what we really need. When Designing for Engagement this level is where the rubber really meets the road.

Level 5: Being Coachable and Coaching Others

The move to this level is a natural outcome of the previous. When you commit to make something happen you move towards its happening and you open the question of it not happening. As we all know when making commitments, about the only thing you know for sure is that how it goes may not be predictable. So when it isn't going the way you predicted, when your assumptions prove to be flawed and your plans don't work, you will likely need a coach. When someone isn't delivering what they said they would, it may be time for coaching. Here are some of the elements of this level.

Being Coachable:
- Inviting support
- Saying what you are up to
- Being accountable
- Being responsible
- Being open to another's contribution

Coaching Others:
- Saying what you are up to
- Being responsible
- Making offers
- Holding others to account
- Committing to another's success

As quickly as I have run through these levels, I want to slow down now and give each one its due discussion, and focus on some how-to in each.

I have looked at a lot of literature over the past twenty-seven years. I am a junkie for new ideas and new ways to present concepts. However, in everything I've read I am almost always left with the question, How do I implement what I have just read? Where's the how-to? The next several chapters will give you plenty of how-to, which will sometimes call on you to be your own best friend, coach, career counselor and life transformer. I will offer you the best tools I know to get you up and standing on your own two feet. I will also remind you that the tools are only that: tools. If you do not at the same time recognize that you need to alter the way you "be" at each level, you will likely be disappointed with the outcomes. Are you ready?

9

Recognizing Myself

Do I know enough about myself to know what I
need from others? Do I know enough about myself
to know what I have to offer others?

*You can search the entire universe for someone more
deserving of your love and affection than you are
yourself and you won't find that person anywhere.*
    Siddhartha Gautama, the Buddha Sakyamuni

Recognize: *verb,* to perceive as existing or true; to
acknowledge or treat as valid

Until you recognize that there is a lot more to you than
the physical space you take up, there can be no real
relationship between you and the newly flattened earth,
you and the world of work, or you and yourself, for that
matter. Most of us do not develop this awareness until later
in life, often after we have missed significant opportunities to accomplish what we intend or contribute to others
in our life. However, with practice and commitment it is
possible to develop an awareness of yourself much earlier.
Maybe we can begin right now while you're still wondering why you'd want to go to the effort.

*Whatever it is that makes up you may well be better
known to others in your life than it is to yourself.*
                                                    Anon.

To begin the practice of Designing for Engagement
you must acknowledge that the first responsibility you have
in this lifetime is to yourself. Charles Handy echoes this
phrase throughout his recent work, *The Hungry Spirit.* He
uses the term "proper selfishness." As Mr. Handy uses it,
it is a kind of view of oneself in relationship to the world:

*What I term a proper selfishness builds on the fact
the we are inevitably intertwined with others, even if
sometimes we wish we weren't, but accepts that it's
proper to be concerned with ourselves and to search
for who we really are, because that search should
lead us to realize that self respect, in the end, only
comes from responsibility, responsibility for other
people and other things.*
                        Charles Handy, *The Hungry Spirit*

In the search for yourself you observe the way you go
about getting things done, the things that really matter to
you to accomplish in this lifetime, your own purpose—and
what it is that you want to dedicate your life to, if you do.
In other words, Recognizing Yourself. In using the term
"recognize" I mean to validate, to witness and appreciate
yourself. This chapter will offer some thoughts on how to
begin that process, if you not yet begun, and how to proceed once you have begun. I say "proceed" because there is
no ending, only a lifelong intention to continue discovering
and appreciating yourself.

*To succeed in this new world, we will have to learn,
first, who we are. Few people, even highly successful ·
people, can answer the questions, "Do you know*

what you are good at? Do you know what you need to learn to get the full benefit of your strengths?" Few have even asked themselves the question.
Peter Drucker, *Leader to Leader,* Spring 2000

Why in 2000 was the then-acknowledged pre-eminent thinker in matters related to management speaking to us of the need to develop an understanding of ourselves? Quite possibly Mr. Drucker's words are not new to you, but almost certainly this was an early occasion for hearing thoughts such as these from a management theorist. Hearing them from a Buddhist teacher would be less surprising; but for a mainstream thinker and writer like Peter Drucker to address the "soft stuff" so directly is nothing short of a breakthrough in thinking.

I have long held the notion that attitudes towards self-exploration and knowledge have been dismissed not because there is no value in the pursuit; rather I believe that as in many other instances in life we make fun of what we do not understand or might leave us vulnerable. It is also simply easier not to know yourself, for a variety of reasons. Abraham Maslow offered these thoughts in 1962 in *Maslow on Management*:

We fear the highest possibilities (as well as our lowest ones). We are generally afraid to become that which we can glimpse in our most perfect moments. We enjoy and even thrill to the godlike possibilities we see in ourselves. And yet we simultaneously shiver with weakness, awe, and fear before these very same possibilities.

Was Maslow saying that we are afraid of ourselves? I think so; and of course one major source of fear is the unknown. My view is that in order to operate effectively in the outsourced economy, the borderless world, whether you are afraid of yourself or not, you must begin the process of Recognizing Yourself.

Note: If you've already noticed that you have a certain way you see the world and that your way of seeing may actually be different from the way the real world is, you are far down the road in the process of "recognizing."

How to begin this practice? Simply sit quietly and listen to yourself talking to you. Some of you will recognize this concept readily. Others may wonder what I am getting at. Just sit quietly and listen for a while; it should become clear in a few minutes. There are many traditions—Zen Buddhism, Tibetan Buddhism, and many others that refer to the practice I am recommending as meditation. For the moment and for my purposes here, all I want is for you to demonstrate to yourself that there is a constant commentary going on in your life as you encounter the world around you. The sound of this commentary is essentially what we think of as "being awake." But those who regularly practice meditation will tell you that listening to the conversation you are having with yourself is far from being awake. Once you get a handle on the fact of this internal dialogue you will notice that it has definite biases. You will also quickly note that it is hard to keep listening because after a few minutes you will begin to think that you are thinking. The truth is, you aren't; the commentary goes on without your assistance.

Recognizing your inner dialogue is a good starting point, but only a starting point. Where is all this chatter coming from? From a place I would name Your Point of View. The one aspect of yourself that may be most difficult to perceive is your own Point of View—how you see the world and the opportunities in it.

It is really more a process than it is a place, but that's making it more complex than it needs to be. Let's just say now that many of our thoughts originate in our Point of View. Let's also say that this process is also the author of and repository for all the chapters of your personal book, titled, *Life, According to Me*, including those refrigerator magnet slogans we carry around with us, like "Life is a scary proposition" or "Life is a blessed opportunity" or whatever version(s) may be your own. The process gives us a predetermined way to respond to what we encounter each moment in life.

It is time to revisit the Recognizing Myself checklist from the previous chapter and take a closer look at some of the practices leading to mastery. Further on, I will be recommending several techniques, or instruments, you can use to assist you in evaluating yourself. I have used these successfully in my consulting practice, and they are readily available if you wish to do your own independent work with this step. It is my hope you will. But first, the checklist:

Recognizing Myself
- Creating My Life Purpose (What am I about?)
- Creating My Life Work and Work Mission (What is my vision?)
- Understanding What Matters to Me (What's my economic Deal?)
- Knowing My Motivators (What is automatically important to me?)
- Understanding My Style (How do I go about getting things done?)
- Knowing My Natural Work (What is the sound of my song?)

Is there more to this? Undoubtedly yes, since this is my own list based on my own personal experience. But it's enough to begin with.

Earlier chapters looked at Life Purpose, Work Mission and Your Economic Deal. Now let's examine the last three elements from my list. What I have to say on each of these topics is far from the last word. Throughout this chapter and at the end of the book, I will be recommending further reading from some other people I consider experts.

In my own Point of View, life really boils down to finding something you love to do, with people you enjoy being with, and doing this work for as long as it satisfies. Work, for me, is simply what someone else is willing to compensate me for in some way; it could be monetarily or in some other fashion as well. Using this definition I would then want to understand what I could do to facilitate the process of getting along in the world so that I could either contribute or sell my work.

If, as stand-on-your-own-two-feet people, we are mostly going to be exchanging our knowledge for value as perceived by others, shouldn't we understand what facilitates that process? What am I to work with? What motivates me in the work environment? What kind of work really turns me on? It always comes back to how well do I Recognize Myself? The answers will begin to show how being successfully related to others is vital to the process of creating value.

Now you've come to an important place in your search for what motivates you, what is your personal style, and "the sound of your song." My best advice is to reach for an instrument.

Instrument: *noun,* 1. a tool to aid with a task; 2. anything that can be used to create music.

There are many instruments of self-evaluation available to us today. The ones I recommend may raise challenges from folks who favor other instruments, or those who would argue against the use of such evaluations at all, believing that they place limitations on people. I am not here to argue with them. My concern is for ease of use and value for your money, since you are going to pursue this on your own. I think once you begin the process of studying yourself in relationship to the world you are probably quite capable of choosing your own instruments. Also, most of us are bright enough to recognize that the information we receive from any form of evaluation is more like a reflection of ourselves than a portrait. It is a glimpse at best, but nonetheless a useful glimpse. You're in charge, don't forget.

Knowing My Motivators
(What is automatically important to me?)
Any work environment involves:
- new ideas and information
- incentives
- responding to others
- leading and following
- doing it the "right (old) way" or doing it a new way
- a relationship to the surroundings and the flow of the work

When it comes to the elements of being at work that can satisfy or dissatisfy, this is a pretty good starting point, though not comprehensive. It is possible to make a case for each of us having needs in these areas, so it is useful to understand how important any of these factors may be to our locating or shaping a satisfying workplace. I recommend a *Personal Interest, Attitudes and Values* instrument offered by Target Training International (TTI) for the purpose of getting information and insight. It is reasonably priced and easy to use.

Understanding My Style
(How do I go about getting things done?)
This is also about how I am perceived by others, how they are affected by me. I am going to recommend the DISC

model, one of the best known behavioral profile models. DISC has been around for years, has gained a lot of acceptance and is particularly valuable because most versions available can be interpreted by a person who is pursuing their own course of self-study. Basically, it reflects your approach to making things happen; i.e., how do you go about it? The model is built on four factors: task orientation, people orientation, pace of work orientation and detail orientation. Each one of us has a Style, which is a mix of all four of these factors. For most of us, one or two factors are reflected strongest. Each DISC instrument uses slightly different descriptive language, but since they are all built on the same model they offer similar output. In my firm, we use the version offered by Target Training. There are other companies making the same offer and a quick search on the web can give you other sources (I have included the contact information for my own firm as well as TTI later in the book). I like DISC because it allows an individual to begin the process of seeing how they are perceived by others. It is most helpful in introducing people to the "self reflective process," providing a basis for understanding, from a behavioral standpoint, how we are going to naturally enter any working situation —because our behaviors have a lot to do with our ability to deliver value.

Knowing My Natural Work
(What is the sound of my song?)
This may be the most controversial aspect of Recognizing Myself, because I am suggesting that each of us has a predisposition to certain types of activities in any field of endeavor. Listen carefully here, because I am saying that the notion that you can be anything you want to be, which is so popular in our culture is a just plain wrong! It is a trap based on a false derivative of the American Dream. We have confused political and civil rights, "all men are created equal" with the laws of nature, which would suggest

otherwise. One of the flaws in this thinking is the insistence on separating ourselves from the natural order of the world we live in, thereby dooming many of us to lives of quiet desperation for what we fail to become. Personally, I have no problem with failing; I've done it lots of times. However, many of us measure ourselves against the shadows of what are considered roles to aspire to in our culture, and never get around to experiencing the joy of being us. This is a true tragedy that affects millions of us.

I am 5'9" and currently 59 years old, in somewhat less than stellar physical condition. Can I aspire to play in the National Basketball Association? Yes. Is it practical or even attainable? No. Why do we persist in telling our children they can be whatever they want to be, when in our hearts we know that is not a true statement? Because, as Maslow suggested, we are afraid of the implications if we aspire to be the best "Us" we could be.

Several years ago, through a career coaching program that I signed up for, I was introduced to the notion that one of my own flaws in thinking as an entrepreneur was that I had to do so many things "Because I Owned the Business!" Our coach was Dan Sullivan. He had learned the hard way, as many of us in the program had, that he was not good at many of the things he worked on in his business, but work on them he did, to the actual detriment of his business. In this program he introduced us to the notion that each of us had a very narrow range of what we were really good at, which contributed most of our value—and then there was all the other stuff, which in reality took away from our optimum contribution. Coming myself from the Be Anything You Want to Be culture, this was a cold slap in the face at first, and then a welcome relief.

Dan Sullivan introduced me to the *Kolbe Index*, the final instrument I am going to recommend. This index gives a person an indication of the kind of work they are going to naturally be drawn to. Not the profession or the subject, but the kind of work. The idea here is that within any profession there are several kinds of work, and we naturally gravitate towards one of them, though we often don't realize it. An easy test of this is to take a look at what is sitting on your desk right now that is not getting done, and that keeps moving to the bottom of the pile. Another test: Note the kinds of meetings you don't want to miss and the ones you would do almost anything to avoid. There is just simply work we love to do and work that is there to be done, and they are not always the same. In this era of virtual mobility the stand-on-your-own-two-feet people will do themselves a big favor by discovering what type of work naturally lights them up, and brings the music with it.

10

Appreciating Interdependence

A broader view of diversity. Meeting the needs
of others. Recognizing your own limitations
and celebrating the strengths of those
we can collaborate with

*A human being is part of the whole called by us
the "Universe," a part limited in time and space.
He experiences himself, his thoughts and feelings as
something separated from the rest—a kind of optical
delusion of consciousness. This delusion is a kind of
prison for us, restricting us to our personal desires and
to affection for a few persons nearest us. Our task must
be to free ourselves from this prison by widening our
circle of compassion to embrace all living creatures and
the whole of nature in its beauty.*

Albert Einstein

There are some subjects that concern us all, but when
you begin to think about them as topics in a book the
first thought that occurs is, "but isn't that just common
sense?" And then upon further reflection the answer comes
back to you that while the subject may be familiar to folks
or commonly talked about, the evidence suggests that it is
anything *but* common sense.

Interdependence may be one of these subjects—the kind of subject that gets blank stares when brought up at a staff or departmental meeting, i.e., "What if we talk about our interdependence with the folks in Marketing?" "Say, I've been thinking that we ought to explore our interdependence with the folks in Human Resources, what do the rest of you think?" Can't you just imagine how such a suggestion might be received in an organization where you are working now? I'm going to hazard a guess that right after the blank stares, when the others in attendance realize you aren't kidding, someone turns loose with a caustic remark about "soft stuff." The ultimate insult in any conversation about organizational performance is to refer to something as soft stuff. As a stand-on-your-own-two-feeter you are going to engage in the practice of mastering the dreaded soft stuff, so you may as well get used to the insults at the outset.

If I may share my reality for a moment—it could be that the only real stuff *is* the soft stuff. I am of the opinion that for many folks in management the greatest disappointment of the new economy is that we are no longer able to "plug and play" people like we did in the machine-age model organizations. When I hear someone get cynical about the issues around being related, what I hear underneath is fear, and I think rightly so. It is fairly apparent that over the years many organizations have demonstrated an amazing ineptitude at supporting their employees in effectively relating to one another in the work environment—much of the ineptitude being on the part of those in leadership/management positions. You should provide your own anecdote here, since it will no doubt be more meaningful than anything I might offer.

With apologies for one more of my consciously long-winded introductions, let's get to the subject of the chapter. Please note that the label I have chosen for this Level of the Design for Engagement is: Appreciating Interdependence, where *appreciating* is the operative term. I could have used *awareness* of interdependence or *accepting* interdependence but I did not because, again, I am encouraging you to take a stronger stand, getting clearer, getting your arms around the idea of interdependence. Earlier I suggested that perhaps the only real stuff is the soft stuff, and then sort of left the statement hanging out there. Here's the rest of that thought: **Interdependence is as real as gravity and, far from being soft, is just as demanding.** When we as a species decide to make friends with the way things work, as we did in the quest for flight, things never before possible *become* possible, familiar, everyday useful. I believe the same holds true for Appreciating Interdependence.

Look what's been happening in the realms of science lately, where increasing amounts of information clearly indicate that the universe we live in is nothing so much as a web of relationships. The "stuff" that we call stuff is not real save for the relationships that keep all of it in existence and of course in plain view. Quite recently, say the past ten years, social scientists and organizational theorists have begun to apply these scientific discoveries to the observation of the behavior of organizations and the people within them. Margaret Wheatley's *Leadership and the New Sciences* and her follow-up, *A Simpler Way*, have found a wide audience among the many folks who are grappling with the challenge of making organizations work, while all around us the rules of workability (if there truly are any) are swirling in this new economy. Early in the 90's Peter Senge's *The Fifth Discipline* introduced us to the notion of systems thinking in an organizational context. It has become popular to talk about systems theory and organizations as organic. Even I like doing it!

But why this groundswell of interest in how the sciences shed light on the inner workings of organizations? Why now? You may recall that the words I have been quoting from Maslow were created over thirty years ago. When his book first came out it was not extremely popular and didn't gain a wide audience, yet much of what he had to say is as fresh today as if it had just been offered. I think it comes down to nothing more profound than PAIN—the pain of massive change and how to cope with it. At this moment in history the pain level is very high, despite the boom in economic outcomes. We are hurting and we are running scared because it is time to understand the world anew, and both the FEAR and the PAIN extend to the highest levels in most organizations. Ironically, it may well be that the precipitators of pain turn out to be the day-to-day breakthroughs that are now so commonplace in information technology.

The upside of this newest technology is a tremendous increase in the potential for individual productivity. The downside (and I use this term in a relative sense for those still in search of control) is the newly created independence of the individual from traditional bureaucracies. The new technology has a voracious appetite and it feeds on bureaucratic tendencies. The net of all this, I believe, will be to free us of the artificial controls of bureaucracy and place us face-to-face with our natural interdependencies—and we are not ready for it!

Honestly, I think it is impossible to accurately study individual behavior separate and apart from the organization/system in which it is occurring. The variables are multitude and there is no such thing as a controlled environment. However, I do believe that an individual can observe his or her behavior in relationship to the many organizational factors, and that same individual can affect change in their behavior, and work to produce change in the behavior of others. Peter Block many years ago in his now-classic book, *The Empowered Manager*, spoke to the notion of developing an awareness of "the world we could affect" within an organization. Block's coaching is extremely useful to anyone, whether manager or not, who has the desire to be even the least bit responsible for the environment in which they participate. Even before that, though, there is a step which only an individual can take.

It starts with an acceptance that we are participants in this web of relationships, as much as any other creature on this planet. Scientists are making this increasingly obvious. This acceptance may have to come as an act of faith since we all suffer from the handicap of being human; our shared dilemma is that we see the world only through our own point of view. Our point of view, our own personal window on the world, would have us see otherwise; it would set us apart. In many ways our point of view would have us see the world as a great pinball game, with us as one ball among many others out on the field at the same time. The way we navigate in this type of reality is up to us; do we carom off the other balls or the bumpers on our way to any destination? Perhaps our adaptation in this reality is to be an aggressive ball and we just blast through any other obstacle that stands in our way. Or maybe we take a defensive tack and derive our motion from being bounced, or driven about the game's surface. In either event we are not in any intrinsic way connected to the other balls except as a result of the outward motions. In truth, this reality is only a function of perception. When it involves people we care for personally, the harsh nature of a pinball game gives way to something much softer, and we acknowledge and nurture the connections. Remember, Einstein called separateness a delusion and a prison, and he knew a thing or two about the bigger picture.

Our own recognition of these connections is probably more qualitative than quantitative. We can more readily witness, and perhaps experience, the degrees of relationship in people we work closely with. If we had the tools we could even measure the impact on us of people we didn't even know or ever see. Now I'm going to give you another way to proceed; it is less precise than a science, and it is going to take an act of faith on the part of many.

This process involves two things: operating from that attitude of meekness I spoke of in Chapter Six, coupled with the declaration offered by Dan Sullivan, **"I am now and forever solely responsible for my own financial welfare. I shall expect no return in life until I have first delivered value to another."**

If you are willing to give this a fair chance, we can truly begin the journey. I am going to take this declaration from Mr. Sullivan and re-name it The Declaration of Inter-dependence. For you to voluntarily adopt both the attitude of meekness and the point of view of interdependence may seem very awkward at first, but day by day you will begin to process the information you receive from the world differently, and your actions will naturally begin to change.

Since you have chosen to work in an organizational setting, you might now consider that the quality of your working relationships is an opportunity or avenue, one way to measure your power in the environment. I am going to remind you here that what I am posing is based on my personal experience and I am looking for you to provide the data for my thesis. It is my strongly held belief that an individual builds organizational power with each and every interaction with the people they work with. At the end of any exchange, the other person(s) must at a minimum be left value-neutral and hopefully value-positive. In other words, they should be looking forward to the next time they have an opportunity to interact with you. This stands in contrast to the experience many of us are familiar with in daily work, where as an outcome of interacting with a co-worker it seems as though we have passed through a toll booth. We got through but we paid a price! Eventually we begin to look for other routes.

So what's next as far as the practice or discipline of Appreciating Interdependence? The practice at this level involves consciously getting to know what the people you interact with need from you—which depends on your being able to understand and communicate what you need.

In the normal course of events when we join a work setting we get to know our co-workers in private; actually, this is the way we get to know most people. As we move from new to familiar we create a mental file on each co-worker. Before we even enter the situation we already have a set of ready-made templates against which we compare everyone, provided very neatly and on file, courtesy of our Point of View. No extra charge, this feature comes with every model. Within some period of time we have everyone sorted out to our satisfaction and we settle in. Jim is like this, Sally is like that, and so on. Unfortunately, the process is conducted completely in private and there is no checking out the assumptions we are making because for the most part we are unaware that the process is going on. Again, no extra charge, this feature is on all basic models.

The practice of Appreciating Interdependence involves the conscious act of breaking the grip of this tendency to pigeon-hole people. In the last chapter I urged you to get to know your own needs. Creating an opportunity to communicate these needs, in the context of your work, is the occasion to get to know the needs of others. How formal this kind of conversation is depends on the degree of interaction you will be having with the other person. Stephen Covey suggests that "we seek first to understand, then to be understood." His coaching applies in this situation perfectly. I may only need to have a five-minute conversation with someone to accomplish my mission, but in those five minutes I can easily learn what they need from me and convey the same to them—if I am intentional about it.

Once a conversation is complete, I need to set my mind to delivering the goods as they have been specified. Over time, if I can consciously deliver to folks what they need, I believe they will do the same for me—and when push comes to shove, as it always does, I will have an account to draw on for that extra fast delivery.

As you know so well by now, this model is drawn from my experience, as are these suggested behaviors. Let me here provide us another quote from one of those credible sources we all like. In this instance I have to give credit to a dear friend, Marcus Robinson, creator of Ethos Channel, and Margaret Wheatley for introducing me to the work of Fred Allen Wolf. Fred is a physicist. I heard him speak at a conference a couple of years back, hosted by Marcus Robinson, and though he doesn't know it, I was very affected by his ability to translate the often complex world of the physicist into terms I could appreciate and use. Here are some words from Fred, lifted from Margaret Wheatley's *Leadership and the New Science*.

I've been saying that meekness is a pathway and my point of view lights the path. Here's how Fred Allen Wolf says it:

> *If the world exists and is not objectively solid and pre-existing before I come on the scene, then what is it? The best answer seems to be that the world is only a potential and not present without me or you to observe it. It is in essence, a ghost world that pops into solid existence each time one of us observes it. All of the world's many events are potentially present, able to be but not actually seen or felt until one of us sees or feels.*

From that I can tell you that in my world—the world of potential—the people I work with want to contribute and be contributed to...because I say so, and that is the way it "pops" into existence for me. I invite you to say something similar for yourself and then act on what you say.

11

Generating Connections

Connecting beyond what you have inherited.
Leveraging differences. How do you get connected?
How do you stay there?

O K, now we are going to step things up a bit. I've had
you looking at your needs in the workplace and finding out about the needs of others. So far you have had to
imagine or create your own needs and learn about those
of your co-workers. Now I am going to ask you to cross
over another line.

Most of us do not have the opportunity to choose the
people we work with; that is to say we are not involved
in the selection or placement process which brings new
folks into an organization. While this may not be altogether
true—I am aware that in certain organizations self-directing
team members do make their own selection decisions—it is
true enough for my purposes, so I will proceed.

We inherit the people we work with and they the same
with us. Inherit, just like your grandmother passed away
and left you her trunk in the attic. The trunk is yours and
so is what is inside. If there is good stuff within, more's the
better; and if not, oh well, we make the best of it. Maybe
we could throw a piece of fabric over that trunk and with
some flowers it would make a nice end table. Or maybe the

kids could use it to store their toys. We make the best of it, whatever is inside. This is something we as humans are very good at, adapting to the situations we find ourselves in and the people we find ourselves with, especially in the workplace. We could complain, and we know some folks do, but in the end the folks we find ourselves working with come back each morning just like we do.

If you have begun to Recognize Yourself and Appreciate Interdependence you may be ready to take on Generating Connections. Why this is crossing over a line is because I'm going to suggest that you add a new dimension of responsibility to your practice of Designing for Engagement.

This is definitely advanced work because now, instead of merely working with the relationships you have inherited, I am suggesting that you co-create them to be what you want them to be—in fact, maybe even *more* than they were intended to be. This will go well beyond discovering the needs of others and communicating your own. At this advanced level you will begin a process of co-creation with fellow workers. In this process of co-creation (very soft stuff, don't you agree?) you will actually be consciously designing working relationships to be more than they would otherwise be. This is a first stage of self-management.

The flow of decisions in most organizations still operates with a vertical orientation: Someone else in some sort of hierarchical structure may be making choices that affect us directly, like what products and services our business is providing. So that part is not up to us or our co-workers to decide upon. This is beyond our span of control, so just like anything else beyond our control we let it be and focus on what we *can* affect. I am going to push you here to imagine that you can affect much more than your point of view would tell you is possible.

My experience in organizations tells me that people

can do just that; they can affect much more than they believe and adapt far more than they need to. As a self-manager you take on the mantle of change, so it is up to you to explore the boundaries for your own satisfaction (appropriate selfishness, as Mr. Handy would say), if for no other reason. But you will not if you are afraid of what you see in front you, or if it looks solid and impenetrable. I have been a consultant to many organizations where results were not happening as desired, and the folks there told me that their hands were tied because the dreaded boundaries of who reports to whom and departmental responsibilities simply would not permit them to do the right thing. Adapting is laudable behavior in a blizzard because you are faced with real circumstances. Adapting to what you *imagine* is not equally worthy of praise. These people were victims of their own perception and quite frequently had never tested their own assumptions or the company folklore.

Now you have to remember that you are being preached at here by a guy who in his corporate working career set a record that still stands, for the most times called into the president's office for reprimand and not getting fired. What can I say? I was young, I was brash and full of principles and, truthfully, lacking in interpersonal skills and too dumb to know better.

I am going to recommend that you take a far different path far from my own. The way I went about my business was much too painful to recommend to anyone. But at least I can tell you why I did it the way I did. I was compensating for a lack of interpersonal skills and at the time being unaware of the rigidity of my own point of view—holding people to standards of behavior that they had never agreed to or, worse yet, imagining their motivation to be less than honorable. Despite the righteousness of my quixotic approach, I probably did as much damage as good in those early years.

Witness your own life for a moment and see if this fits. If your life has rolled out in the scenario I suggested earlier—you were born, you grew up, found something to do that you love with people you care about, etc, and at some point you were involved in an educational process. You received some certification or degree and marched out into the world to seek your fortune. There you were, all full of knowledge and stuff, suddenly confronted with the growing awareness that despite all your knowledge there may have been some fundamental human skill missing and it was the key to everything: the ability to negotiate, advocate and collaborate. I am not talking about negotiate or advocate in the classic win/lose full of testosterone sense. I mean negotiate so everybody wins. Advocate to be understood, not dominate; collaborate as a means to effectiveness; the abilities needed for engaging in productive dialogue. These were not courses offered in any curriculum I can recall. We did not study this skill. I do remember that on my report cards throughout Catholic elementary school we got a grade each marking period for something called, "works and plays well with others," but there was no class on this subject and I think we were mostly getting graded for not hitting each other during recess.

At this point in life most of us are going on our own experience (let's call it auto-pilot), coupled with our own ignorance, and doing the best we can to negotiate for what we want as the need arises—too often with poor results. Sure, there are people who are good at the dialogue process, but this ability does not appear to be very evenly distributed across the working population. So those who do have the ability move ahead and those who don't, brilliant or otherwise, languish.

But the skills can be learned—and you can teach yourself. The more important question is: Do you really want to develop the skills? Do you have sufficient cause to place yourself in a learning mode and perhaps take several months to develop proficiency? If your answer is yes, then as an excellent proven guide to developing these skills I recommend the book, *Crucial Conversations*, by Joseph Grenny et al. As a how-to, it is in a class by itself. Joseph Grenny and his partners have spent nearly twenty-five years developing a methodology for practical application in any working environment.

So, what about your dialogue skills? Are you able to advocate on your own behalf and not burn bridges in the process? Can you listen to heated or tense conversations without taking things personally? When someone acts in a surprising, negative manner, do you jump to conclusions, or are you able to give them the benefit of the doubt, and probe in a non-threatening way to discover their motivation? If you are like me, your answer is probably "sometimes" to all these questions. The need for developing confidence in your dialogue skills is not something to apologize for, it has become a necessity in the outsourced economy.

If you have accepted my fundamental thesis about interdependence, then you are probably increasingly aware that not all the relationships you have or will inherit have the strength or qualities you need. One of the things you need right from the get-go is to know from the other person "what they are all about." I think this is consistent with what Stephen Covey refers to as "seeking first to understand, then to be understood." Remember always that this is a working-together context, so when I say, "what they are all about," I am wanting to get at, 1) *what* they are trying to accomplish, 2) *how* they are trying to accomplish it, and 3) *why* they are trying to accomplish it.

This goes well beyond mere results and into what the other person is trying to learn as they move ahead, and what future state they want to arrive at. So you are really working to get to know this person as their *working commitments*, not simply as a personality or a set of competencies.

111

Questions like: Why have they chosen to work here? Where are they planning to go with their career? Is there anything specific they are trying to accomplish while getting their work done? I believe that without this level of Engagement you cannot fully serve the folks who serve you.

On the other hand, the most common and well developed set of communication skills you will see in the workplace involves defending ourselves or attacking someone else—our basic survival skills to keep us safe from harm or destroy our enemies. Whenever we encounter a situation at work that seems somewhat threatening, these communication habits kick into high gear and remain in gear until the perceived threat abates. I can't imagine that I have to do a whole lot of explanation here because we all know these situations. The vast majority of these perceived threats involve no real danger to life or limb, but they do seem to threaten either our work getting done, our position in the enterprise or some loss of face or status.

Because we lack the ability to get or remain centered in these encounters, we can easily feel under attack or out of control, and we scramble verbally to regain our balance. This can happen even with close associates, as you can probably attest to. After a certain number of these exchanges we start adapting to our own limitations, making the best of it. Our behaviors become some combination of avoidance and rationalization for actions not taken. Excuses may become handy; "I tried that before, it'll never work"..."She's not going to help with that, she'll just tell me how busy she is." Often times these conversations take place only with ourselves. Why bother with the nasty business of confrontation if you can have both sides of the conversation in your head and save everyone from being uncomfortable?

Sometimes it is not even an actual threat that is present. We may be faced with a situation where the relationship we have with a co-worker is sufficient but we need it to be great, or at least better. Then the thought of approaching the topic with our co-worker causes our own imagination to kick in and provide a picture that suggests confrontation, and we don't want that. We don't want that *so much* that the conversation never takes place and we lose, our co-worker loses and our enterprise loses, all at the same time.

If you are going to move successfully into and dwell in this level of Designing for Engagement you will need to have some mastery of Appreciating Interdependence— seeing the world you work in as mutually beneficial and mutually dependent. From that understanding you will be able to recognize and confront your inability to communicate in stressful situations. This is an instance where you use the pain to your advantage.

Here are the potential pitfalls in any conversation that attempts to cause work to occur: 1) failure to establish or maintain mutual purpose, 2) failure to establish or maintain mutual respect, and 3) failure to arrive at shared understanding.

See, this isn't rocket science from a conceptual standpoint, but the trick is to stay conscious when the going gets tough, because you *will* fail at this, even after you learn the skills. The real question for each of us will be can we continue in the face of our own failure. I say yes, if we can keep reminding ourselves of what the stakes are. I will be the first to say that sometimes the pain is not worth the gain; I see very little future in being a human sacrifice in the workplace, but you will always have to be the judge of that, and in the end answer only to yourself.

I am going to remind you that Generating Connections is about giving up those old habits of somehow just "surviving" the conversation, and instead working towards what you see as possible and necessary. I am going to submit that you are going to survive anyway. In this hot economy good people shouldn't have to put up with much of what they don't want. The question for you, then, is: Do you want to take on the opportunity of shaping your working environment? Do you want to take on *being* the changes you want to see happen?

12

Taking Effective Action

Building value through competence, collaboration and good reputation

We have arrived at the point where the rubber finally begins to meet the road. Taking Effective Action is how all employers want their folks to be related all of the time. They may not see it as a Level of Engagement or say it the way I do, but if you ask you will quickly get something similar for an answer. And why not? This is where the work gets delivered, this is where the Return on Investment shows up, and this is what the game is all about. And if people were mechanical parts, this is where we would start, each day—simply flip the switch and let the machine run as fast and hard as it could.

We know, however, that we are not machines but sometimes, based on the conversations we get into, we wonder if our managers and some of our co-workers realize this, and sometimes our own behavior should be called into question. I was conducting a workshop recently and in the process of sharing something on a particularly tough topic, one of the participants began to weep while speaking. I have no problem with this kind of self-expression, but apparently some people did. On the evaluations for the session, a participant took the time to let me know they thought the expression of emotion was very unprofessional; they went further and asked in the future that I not promote that kind of thing! So now I know...professional includes being unemotional. Leave that part of your humanity at the door on your way into work. After all, it hasn't been that long that we have been asking people to only bring their brains to work, so I guess I just need to be a bit more patient, very unemotionally patient. Interesting isn't it, weeping is considered unprofessional but many of our past revered leaders and even many today quite readily express anger, and I never hear anyone describe that as unprofessional. Some people just need to express anger to be effective. We all know that, and of course we all know that tears are a sign of ineffectiveness.

Ah me, how I rant. But back to the topic, Taking Effective Action. Having chosen to operate as a stand-on-your-own-two-feeter, this Level of Engagement should be of great interest, because here is where you deliver value and create an audience for your voice; and here also is where you establish the possibility for realizing your reward in financial as well as other terms. Can you take effective action without mastering the previous levels of Design? I believe so, at least some of the time, but the matter is one of delivering value consistently over time, in varying circumstances and with diverse groups of people. This is a much more ticklish proposition, one that lends itself to a great deal of unpredictability—therefore, the need for skill and perceptiveness.

If you are this far into the book and still paying attention you know that performance in an organizational setting is not an individual phenomenon. In those years of my personal corporate performance, I had occasion to be considered a top performer in one environment, worthy of termination in another, a solid team member in a third and a hot shot in my final assignment. How do we explain all that? I was the same person in all four assignments; however, during that second job assignment I could not find an effective way to work with my internal clients and co-workers and it cost me, both personally and professionally. I was passed over for an annual merit increase and my confidence took a tumble at the same time. Clearly, too much weight is given to the individual in the performance equation, especially as it relates to compensation.

But why do I think Taking Effective Action qualifies as a Level of Engagement? This notion suggests a state of readiness or potential. Let's say that the potential for performance in an organizational setting could be represented by this formula: **Technical Competence + Collaborative Skill + Good Reputation = Potential Performance** (a variant on my earlier Adaptability Index). I am saying it is possible to be related in a state of readiness to Take Effective Action, and it requires *consciousness*.

Imagine, because this is my favorite example, that in considering organizational performance you saw yourself as a member of a trapeze act as an aerial artist.. There may be more precision situations but this one definitely qualifies. Each member of one of these teams must be in a constant state of preparedness and on hand for each night's performance. But simply showing up each night is far from enough to get through the show. Before someone is allowed to participate in this setting they must have already demonstrated sufficient technical competence, but that competence must be constantly maintained; any competence is subject to atrophy and the more insidious "assumptivitis syndrome." This syndrome affects anyone who does not regularly check the status of the skills that make up a competence, except as a matter of memory. Ridden a bike recently?

Haven't we all heard the saying, "It's just like riding a bicycle, once you learn you never forget." I recently began riding a bicycle after a gap in practice of about thirty years. Could I still ride? Yes I could, but it wasn't the way I recalled doing it. I vividly remembered jumping curbs with abandon, riding with no hands, looking forward to blazing down treacherous hills, the more treacherous the better—until my son offered me my first off-road experience recently. I am happy to report that there was no one or nothing riding on the relationship of my competence to my memory...well, except my pride of course.

It may not be obvious, and yet I ask you to consider that Collaborative Skills, along with Technical Competence, also play a part in the aerial performance, as each performer must be able to express themselves clearly and precisely, in a timely manner without misunderstandings, and listen in the same manner.

Finally, there is the factor I call Good Reputation. I'll spend a bit more time with this later, but for now let's see if you can be satisfied with understanding that much of your ability to move without constraint in an organization is a function of your Good Reputation, which results in a certain Field of Trust building around you. In some cases this is personal trust but most often it is professional trust, and it is like money in the bank. This Field of Trust acts like a non-stick coating, allowing you to flow smoothly through organizational waters that others find choppy and filled with snags.

Good Reputation builds, one conversation at a time, but it has exponential implications in that where you have built a Good Reputation you can usually count on it being spread as a possibility, further reducing friction in future interactions with both old and new co-workers, and reducing the amount of energy you have to expend for each accomplishment. As you probably realize, the same principles hold true in the negative as well. Being shortsighted in your interactions with people can quickly build you a poor reputation. Unfortunately, I think the vast majority of people in the workplace have "No Reputation," which may well be the worst case. This is to say that folks don't recognize reputation as currency so they pay little attention to its construction and maintenance. The issues surrounding reputation obviously hold true at the level of the organization as well. I would go so far as to say the Good or Poor Reputation of any company is the sum of the reputations of the people who interact with its customers.

Back now to the circus tent. How would you like to be working the trapeze as the person who does the jumping and flipping, and find yourself winding up in the net 20-30% of the time? Well first off, it would probably not be very pleasant, net burns on your face and all. Secondly, with that percentage of misses there begins to be doubt in your mind and those of your teammates and it affects everyone's performance too. Thirdly, even though the act is beautiful to watch, one of its primary attractions is the danger of a fall. But the audience is not paying to see the fact of the fall, they are paying for the opportunity to get all worked up and then relieved and thrilled as the catches are made. If you are in the net 20-30% of the time, there is no one in the seats, word gets around; remember, Good Reputation counts and is much easier to build than repair.

Yes, yes, yes, I know the vast majority of us are not or never will work the high acts in the circus. Moreover, we are used to being valued on an individual basis. We wouldn't begin to think we could get away with such a shoddy set of performances as the ones offered by our friends on the trapeze. But let's say you are a member of a project team charged with getting a new product to market...and you have slipped the due date on the product four times and are working on a fifth. You know this example, right? You've been there, maybe you are there right now. Why is anybody still paying you and your team members, why haven't you been replaced? Why are there still people in the audience?

Remember I said earlier we don't have enough sensitivity to how we are affected by others, or how we are affecting them; we also do not have very much sensitivity to the performance of groups of people, as they are in action. We may be part of the project team but chances are better than good that our performance is being evaluated individually. Oh, someone will hang for the slipped dates— the project manager; the fourth project manager to be specific. This example also has systemic implications that go well beyond the scope of what I am addressing here. If you are or have been in this position you must have made the same observations as I am sharing here and asked yourself the same questions. I think all of us know the truth of the situation and nobody talks about it openly.

The truth? When these project plans and due dates get put together we're just guessing, mostly based on past experience! The whole notion of project planning is for the most part mechanical while the project itself is entirely organic, which is to say unpredictable. Because we use mechanical planning models that do not account for performance differences we assume uniform technical competence. In a mechanical world an engineer is an engineer and a programmer is a programmer and head count rules. Here's what I think: The relationship between "headcount theory" and reality is about as close as "flat" is to the shape of this planet.

Just between us stand-on-your-own-two-feet types, if you are working in an organization that relies heavily on Head Count Management practices, you are in an environment that is not suitable for human habitation and it is time to dust off the old resume and dial up The Dice.com. I mean do not even think twice, just head for the door. You are employed in a business run by crazy people!

I am willing to bet a lot that in the practice of creating most project plans, process documentation substitutes for collaborative skill (Who designs most project management tools? Engineers, and they do not have tools that account for bad days, sick children and variances in abilities. How about their interpersonal skills?), while the resident technical competence, much like my bike riding skill, is assumed as a constant. Actually, I believe it is more than assumed, it is counted on. We are, as my son would say, "so" counting on the assumed technical competence to save the day that we completely devalue the collaborative skill component of performance, and Good Reputation is sacrificed to the gods of Hope.

Here's another example from the rich tapestry which is my past. Have you ever heard the saying, "Even a one-eyed man could be King in the land of the blind?" Being a "one-eyed man" was sort of how I began my business nineteen years ago. I could see the role collaborative skills played in organizational performance and the value of Good Reputation, but many of my clients were still operating in the darkness of simple talent as the answer to performance—oh, and enough budget of course, in case talent didn't carry the day.

One client in particular was particularly guilty of "assumptivitis" as well as suffering with a near terminal case of What-About-Our-Glorious-Past-amundo? The consequence of the combination of these two maladies was a sort of paralysis that took the form of the place having the feel of trying to walk in a vat of molasses. Interestingly, the paralysis was only noticeable if you came into the organization from the outside. If you worked there you thought everything was fine and the whole world moved that slowly. When called upon to work on the then-hot project, which was of course late, very late, we were asked by the client to evaluate the viability of their development process. This was the early 90's and the standard diagnosis for everything by then was "broken process," and the usual prescription was "re-engineering." We asked the client if rather than consider re-engineering as a first alternative, could we just observe the team at work for a short while. This was of course cheaper, so the client consented. It did not take us long to discover that what we were faced with was a very bright, very committed, very mis-aligned and very frustrated group of people who were, by word of mouth, rapidly making their workplace, "so not the place to be." These folks weren't too happy to see us, either.

By poking about, asking questions and watching team meetings it soon became apparent to us (the one-eyed guys) that our client was blinded by a fairly simple fact. With each new project the Marketing people would consult the customer and determine product specifications. These product specifications would then be discussed in the obligatory full team meeting; and then the Development guys would tell the Marketing guys that they could design the product and the Manufacturing guys would tell everyone that they could make the product. Then the Marketing guys would go to the customer and tell them that they were going to get what they wanted and give them a delivery date. And then everyone, Development, Manufacturing and Marketing would begin the process of being late, without realizing it. The Development guys would go back to their labs and begin taking as long as it took to bring the customer a truly elegant solution, never mind that elegance was not in the product specification set. The Manufacturing guys would go back to their site and immediately add four months to whatever the Development guys had given them as a delivery date, and that was written in pencil.

An important feature of this relationship was that the Manufacturing guys never told the Development guys what they were doing and the Development guys never divulged their commitment to elegance to anyone. It was like both groups operated inside a cone of silence. They could see each other but they had no idea what was really going on. As to Reputation, I am sure you can imagine. Meanwhile, the Marketing guys would have to stand by and develop ulcers, since they had no clout in the process, and needed to make up a series of excuses for the customer and watch the market share drop by one full point each year over a ten-year period—point by point as the broken development process repeated itself year after year.

All the elements of what I have been talking about are included in this story, except for mentioning that the only way this situation could have persisted as long as it did was the organization's tolerance for PAIN—and a conspiracy of silence on the part of all concerned. These folks clearly did not understand the necessity of interdependent behavior; the idea of Generating Connections across departmental lines was a foreign subject. So when it came time for Taking Effective Action, what they had going for them was an abundance of technical competence and a hope in the patience of the marketplace.

Fortunately, the story has a happy ending or I would probably not be sharing it with you. On our recommendation the client allowed us to conduct a series of workshops with everyone on the project team involved. This cost the business more in terms of time away from the workplace than it did in our fees, but the time turned out to be well spent. During the course of the workshops we were able to have all parties begin to see their complicity and responsibility for the situation, own up to their lack of collaborative skills and lack of concern for Good Reputation and commit to acting on behalf of the Greater Good. The net of all the conversations was that the commitment made to the customer became the driver of the process (Good Reputation), and technical elegance, while important, had to become a secondary concern. Since the technical competence required was in place, it then fell to us to coach folks as they worked in developing the necessary collaborative skills and concern for Good Reputation. I have to be honest and tell you that their level of pain helped move the process along too, but there must be either PAIN or DESIRE to bring about change, and you work with what you got!

Eight months after we came on the scene this team delivered the product to the customer at the time they said they would, as promised, within budget and with higher quality measures than ever recorded. As a replacement for technical elegance, the team had embraced the customer as integral to the entire process. Following this project this same group of folks took on another new offering, and with much less of our assistance cut more time from their process, as well as cut budget expended, and continued to increase the quality of the finished product. We continued in a minor role for a third project and the team continued to improve. At the end of three years we completed our relationship with this group. Market share had improved dramatically during this period, new team members were being oriented to this team's way of working as soon as they joined, and this working department had become "the place to be."

Returning to the image of the trapeze: Long before the drop rate gets to 20% you are in communication with your partner, the catcher. In an initial conversation you discover that your catcher has been silently suffering with tendonitis. This ailment has weakened his gripping power (let's go with a guy catcher, OK?) but because he fears for his job, he has not said anything (verbally, that is). This is an example where there is a problem with technical competence and the concern for Good Reputation has been displaced by something else. This is not a bad person, this is just someone working from an ordinary context of self-concern, not recognizing the relationship he needs to have with you and that you need from him. Your catcher has lost touch with the Greater Good and has forgotten that it is his Good Reputation that allows you to perform at your best. He is stuck in a swirl of self-concern.

At the point of Taking Effective Action you must be related to those who rely on you, just like you were a part of the trapeze act. You have to be prepared to deliver (technically competent), prepared to communicate (skilled collaboratively), and understand that the Greater Good demands Good Reputation. Simply put, if you cannot do what is requested, don't say you will. If you say you will, be willing to move heaven and earth to make it happen. If you discover, for whatever reason, that you aren't going to be able to deliver, let whoever is counting on you know so they can make adjustments. At the same time, let those with whom you work come to understand that this is the only way you want to work—as if it really matters, like you are playing for keeps. When my wife used to work with my company as a consultant she was fond of saying to the client, "Listen, you better act like it matters, 'cause otherwise you are just making Barbie Dolls!" I actually think that hurt some people's feelings.

The bottom line here, keep your skills up to date and be in a learning process at all times. Learn the needed Collaborative Skills and practice, practice. Finally, never forget that Good Reputation is essential to performance. Pay attention to your own Reputation but insist that others manage theirs with you as well.

13

Being Coachable

We are not perfect; we will experience
disappointment and failures. How to remain open to
the experience and support
of those around us

*Play for keeps, as children do...remember, it's just
the Games Big People Play.*

MFC 4/06/06

Now as is my habit, it will take me a while to get to
the point here. If you have been patient with me so
far you have seen that I have to sort of talk my way to the
bottom line, I can't just go there.

I know it is about money and your family's welfare
and all that; employment, I mean. You might recall that at
the beginning of the book I said it had to be about results
or it wouldn't be worth talking about—and so it is all
about risk as well. When it comes to the topics of results
and risk, my greatest interest is in working with folks who
are really up to something, as opposed to minimizing their
exposure, so these two factors, results and risk, must be
part of the conversation. When folks are demonstrating
that they really are up to something, I am very interested,

will make big commitments, and will play very hard. The thing I like least about being "grown up" is that people stop playing for keeps and start being careful. They also begin taking everything and especially themselves seriously. I believe this to be a function of having abdicated a portion of the responsibility for your future into the hands of someone else. Perhaps this type of behavior is a carryover from the Age of Willing Dependency. I can't say for certain, because I wasn't around before the turn of the last century.

Appreciating Interdependence does not have anything to do with giving up responsibility, nor does Generating Connections or Taking Effective Action. In fact, if you have been following the theme here, each of the Levels involved in Designing for Engagement suggests a *greater* degree of responsibility, intentionally relinquishing control, and cultivating an attitude of selfish vulnerability. The "levels" I have been working to distinguish move into and out of view, based entirely on your level of consciousness of what you are up to. If you are ever going to get to be a fully functioning on-your-own-feet kind of person, you will have to operate just like those trapeze artists in the previous chapter. Optimal and appropriate working relationships must become part of your performance equation.

This brings us to another point of paradox. I believe true freedom—as in standing on your own two feet in whatever domain—is paradoxical in nature. If we live in a web of interdependence, then by virtue of that fact, freedom becomes a matter of acceptance, or surrender to the state or condition of interdependence; the **meekness** I referred to earlier.

Being Coachable, an attitude grounded in meekness, becomes both the ultimate source of Power to make things happen, and the key to individual freedom.

The last 100 years of experience in our workplaces

have truly muddied the waters around the concept of freedom. As citizens we have been free, free to choose our leaders, free to make many decisions for ourselves about how we would choose to live, if and how we would choose to practice a religion and other freedoms as well; all on the weekends! But during the better part of each week (once we have made a choice about where to be employed) many of us do not experience the same freedoms. We have been free to choose to relinquish our freedom in exchange for "making a living." The majority of us have made this choice.

In my view, we made this exchange innocently enough, perhaps more expediently than consciously. Historically many of us married young and began our families while we were young, well before we had fully formed any concept of ourselves or our vision. Once present to our responsibilities, we chose to exchange a large portion of our lives for the security of a paycheck. It seemed like a responsible choice to make. Unfortunately, I believe this choice has been incredibly and immeasurably costly to our experience and participation as citizens. Not just citizens in the political sense, but also in the sense of simply watching out for each other.

We as Americans—and now greater numbers of people around the world—have undoubtedly benefited enormously in a material sense, from the perspective of individual freedom of thought, by living in a nation where leaders were elected and affairs of church were kept separate from affairs of state. However, I am not as convinced that we haven't cancelled or nullified much of the idealized benefit of these freedoms by failing to expect it in *all* aspects of our daily lives. Can we say without hesitation that the 25, 35, in some cases 45 years during which we spent 60%-70% of our waking lives in a position of having subordinated our freedom for a paycheck, has really been worth it? Personally, I cannot see that it has been a good deal for our cherished free way of life. What is my evidence? Take this example: According to the U.S. Census Bureau 60% of those citizens eligible to vote in the 2000 Presidential election did so. In terms of numbers of people who did not participate, this means 74 million eligible people did not make the trip to the voting booths, but the mall parking lots all across America are full many weekday evenings and from Saturday morning until Sunday evening! Have we grown numb to the responsibility for our own freedom in exchange for the right to shop? Materially, we have benefited by exempting the behaviors, practices, and conditions within our economic institutions from the freedoms and principles that govern the rest of our lives.

As we shift out of the Age of Willing Dependency into the Age of Standing on Our Own Two Feet, and the balance of opportunity continues to shift to favor the individual over the organization, changes are inevitable; we're starting to see them now. Past employer practices of offering security and a living wage, expecting unquestioned loyalty, placing job before family and other obligations—and other artifacts of a dependent relationship—are giving way to much more participatory or mutually beneficial practices. All this has the potential of making our workplaces more humane habitats, but you and I know that there is yet a ways to go.

Always with an increase of freedom comes an increase of responsibility. Everyone seems to be for the freedom part, and then there are always the questions of readiness and expectations. I cannot remember exactly when we first heard the word Empowerment. I know it would suit me just fine if this was the last time. This concept, which appeared everywhere in the early-to-mid 90's, was first greeted as a breath of the kind of freedom we had all been wanting in our workplaces. Very quickly soon after, I think, it began to be exposed as perhaps one more attempt by the old patriarchy to demonstrate largess. Maybe I am too harsh, I'll let you judge, but were we surprised when managers were not ready to let go of the control they were used to? No! Were we surprised when employees stood around like so many inmates just released from their jail cells upon hearing that they were now Empowered (sorry), wondering what to do with their newly granted freedom? Yes! Fortunately, once again, PAIN came to our assistance.

Midway through the 1990's, with everyone doing their damnedest to have employees (who were creatures of the Age of Willing Dependence) take on more responsibility for decision-making, and with harangues about "attitudes of entitlement" and managers from the same Age doing more to avoid letting go of the decision-making function... a miracle happened. Information technology exploded and global competition became a reality at the very same time. What! No more time to worry as much about management control. "Just Do It" became the marching orders. And within the past ten years we have seen more "freedom to contribute" happening than we could probably have imagined, more out of desperation than design, but who's keeping track of motivation? The important fact is that it is happening.

The marketplace for talent became as tight as a drum in the mid-1990's and people at a very young age, with very big ideas, very few preconceptions or interest about the way organizational life had historically worked were learning that they could name their own game. This period—some might say during the dot-com gold rush—has been followed by the demolition of long-held beliefs. What were they? That the talents needed for many of our knowledge businesses were only resident within our borders, and that certain types of work would always be done here in the United States.

If you had asked many of your friends ten years back whether U.S. Federal Income Tax Returns would be processed in India—well, you probably couldn't have gotten the question out of your mouth before your listeners were either rolling on the floor holding their sides or at your throat wanting to know if you were a "real American." While we were not paying attention, many of us, the education levels in other countries were rising. All it took for the world to go flat was the combination of technical skills and communication technology to have a certain convergence; capitalism took care of the rest. Employment opportunities now began to flood to other parts of the world.

In many ways it is the rest of us who are still catching up. But like all increases in freedom, this one arrives with new responsibilities as well. There is now more economic power available to individuals than there are likely individuals to take advantage of the shift in the balance of power. This is mainly a function of our collective Point of View rather than any formal educational gap. As a workforce we are somewhat stunned at the rapid pace of change, not only in technology but also beliefs. I believe we are at a significant crossroads in the development of both democracy and ourselves as citizens. If we seize the moment we can move the democratic way of life further towards expression than ever in history. Or we could resist the responsibility that is now called for and bond around our woes—turning towards a more directive form of government and way of life and bringing to a close the idea of America. The basic paradox that we will need to navigate is one I might frame as **Standing On Our Own Two Feet...Together**.

I told you I would get to the bottom line eventually. I apologize if that seemed like a long detour. I felt it important to establish that Being Coachable has not necessarily been a by-product of our recent economic experiences. To Be Coachable would seem to be just common sense—that is, until we consider that the makeup of today's workforce is a composition of: 1) **younger people** who have never been told they were anything less than tremendous,

2) among them **minorities** who may or may not have family histories that involved happy organizational experiences, and course, 3) **women,** who are for the most collaborative by nature but may not have large amounts of self confidence, and 4) the **40-and-over** group who are desperately hoping that they can stay employed until their kids get through college. This is not fertile ground for either trust or admitting that you need help of any kind.

Our primary concern in Taking Effective Action is the production of results. If we are not producing results now, we will need to in the future. How will we develop the requisite abilities? Now we will take the process to the next and most senior level. As one who is standing on your own two feet, or is on your way, you are also increasingly going to need to be responsible for professional and career development in your workplace. You will note that I did not limit the statement to "your" professional and career development and for very specific reasons. If we continue to play the interdependence card at every level of the Design for Engagement, then it plays here too.

This final Level of Designing for Engagement I call Being Coachable and Coaching. It is a continuation of operating as if you recognize that your own success is not of your doing alone, nor is others' success a matter of *their* doing exclusively. Mutuality, Interdependence, Win/ Win: They all imply the same thing to me. What is important is the freedom that becomes available when we surrender to this way of operating. This chapter speaks to Being Coachable, the next chapter to Coaching.

You can most likely imagine a situation where you make a commitment to deliver something in your workplace and upon getting into the task discover barriers of one sort or another that look like they will inhibit your ability to deliver as promised. It may not be clear to you exactly the nature of the barriers, or maybe it is, but in either event you know that you are in trouble. I am always going to take you back to the Greater Good and here is another instance. If you can keep yourself clear about the Greater Good you open yourself up to receive the contribution of someone else. My own personal example of this is so etched in my memory that it is easy to share but still painful nonetheless.

When I was thirteen I first encountered basketball as a competitive team sport, distinct from shooting baskets in the backyard. I found that I was really attracted to the team nature of the game, many of my close friends were going to be on our school team and it seemed like something I really wanted to do. However, I had little skill and less knowledge of the game. Consequently, I spent a not-so-fun year sitting on the bench or playing the last two minutes of our games. I think that if more guys had tried out, I would not even have made it to the bench. At the end of the season my coach told my father that it would be good if I didn't try out the next year because he wanted to save me the embarrassment of being cut from the squad. I don't recall why my father did not convey this message until many years later, but I think he knew just how much I wanted to play.

The next year our school had a new basketball coach and I still had a great desire to play. I had worked on my skills during the year, not always getting the flow of the game, but I was better, and I made the team. There was still a question of understanding the game, but I wanted this very badly. My new coach, a man I am still grateful to, played off my desire and would stay with me after practices working on the basics of understanding how the players moved about the court and coordinated their actions. Much to my surprise as well as that of my teammates, everything fell into place all of a sudden and I became a main contributor to the team that year, even getting into the starting rotation for some games. By this time you have probably guessed that I am not a gifted athlete and

134

when the next year came around, my competency, what little I developed, had eroded and it was back to the bench for me. The coach knew I was disappointed and he took me aside and let me know that he was confident that if I would work as hard as I had the previous year, I would get back into the starting lineup before too long. I worked hard and he was right; it paid off for all concerned, as we won our league championship that year for the first time in the history of the school. I was not a star but I was a member of a championship team. I had put aside my concern for myself and in the interest of the Greater Good had the patience to develop under the guidance of this coach. Maybe for the first time in my life something meant so much to me that I was willing to let someone teach me what they knew.

Well, this state of grace didn't last long. I went to high school the next year and by now my skills had actually developed considerably. My knowledge of the game was however, still incomplete. Who knows why we become more interested in being right than in being rich at some points in our lives? I think maybe it isn't so much cockiness, though it looks that way, as it is that we get fixated by our own point of view. In any event, in the space of twelve months I went from being a sponge soaking up every bit of knowledge I could get on how to play basketball to being a know-it-all. I became every coach's worst nightmare, a player with the talent but who was uncoachable. Surprisingly, even sitting the bench was no longer sufficient incentive for me to alter my attitude. By the time I was a senior I was clearly talented enough to be a starting player, but my inattention to what the coach was trying to accomplish led to my going back to the bench, replaced by a sophomore in the starting lineup.

It took me several years to stop stinging from that experience, and even now there is a hint of embarrassment as I tell you the story. What had gone wrong? Remember in the last chapter I said the trick about Taking Effective Action was not doing it once but consistently over time, in a variety of settings. Well, I did not have the benefit of my own insight then. If I did I would have seen that as a basketball player I had, and probably always would have, marginal skills. The willingness I had displayed in my early playing years had overcome these shortcomings, not replaced them. When I became a know-it-all I lost my edge without even realizing it. So I had Minimum Competence without Collaborative Skills and no concept of Good Reputation. I was hoist by my own pitard! I have never seen a pitard but being hoisted by anything can't be good. And from the standpoint of that organization, I was not going to contribute much to the organizational performance. Several years later, after all this had become clear to me, I did play on another championship team. I was not a star there either, but I made a solid contribution and it was very satisfying.

So, on to the principles of Being Coachable, in the present. We are all in this newly flattened world together now, and from what I can see there is more change occurring than any one of us can keep track of, and not enough time to do it even if we could. This means that it is highly likely that we are all going to be faced with not being aware that our ability to deliver the goods is in jeopardy. I mean "the goods" here in the sense that our own material welfare is at risk and our employer needs someone who can do what you do but at a much reduced cost, and they are available! Coming into any workplace armed with this knowledge may make it easier to make the adjustment to Being Coachable by another of our co-workers. But be clear at the outset that you must be responsible for creating this opportunity for yourself. You will do it if you can stay present to working for the Greater Good, and find those around you who want to operate in a similar fashion.

I think I have covered this ground already, but you *do* know it is all going to turn out for you, right? You are reasonably talented, somewhat articulate, properly selfish, your personal hygiene is not a problem for people and you know the score, which is to say that if you don't like it where you are working now, you can move pretty readily as long as you don't trash your reputation. With this as your platform, why not go for having it be as good as it can be? I just don't think there is that much to lose. Besides, the worst thing that can happen is probably something great.

I want to make it clear at the outset that the value of Being Coachable is derived in *equal measure* from your desire as the person being coached, plus the wisdom of the coaching you get. I say this in case you are wondering if you have to find the perfect coach. You don't, since coaching in this context is a way of Being Engaged, not a position.

The real question, the more important one, is do you want to be related to your co-workers this way? You don't have to, there is a real good chance no one is going to ask you to and yet, if you really are going to operate standing on your own two feet, increasing the scope of what you will be responsible for (in this instance, your own development) will play a major part in reducing the occurrence of victimization.

Now what is there to do in Being Coachable? First off, if you have been working on developing some measure of mastery in the other Levels, you have around you a web of very intentionally and powerfully constructed working relationships. Most of the time, when things are going well, we are not in need of the power of these relationships, we are *feeding* them power. It is when the going gets tough and things are not going as planned that we draw on the power we have stored, in order to produce corrective action in service of shared objectives being met.

The first bit of doing is acknowledging to yourself when things are not going as planned.

Pride makes us artifical and humility makes us real.
Thomas Merton

The second bit of doing is to acknowledge the same thing to someone who has some competence in the matter or a stake in your success, preferably both, and is willing to act like it. This is the hardest step in the coaching process because it makes present what we all know and hate to talk about...we really do need each other. Once we are over this emotional hurdle, much of the rest becomes easy. Being Coachable then becomes a process of conversing with someone else to disclose where you are stuck. The nature of the coaching conversation works best if it is an "inquiry" in nature. By "inquiry" I mean something quite different from receiving advice from an expert—that's receiving advice from an expert, not being coached! Seeking advice may at times be valuable but we are assuming that Being Coached is not one of these situations.

The design of a Being Coached conversation is best when the burden is on you to generate your own course of action. In the presence of an expert it's probably best to just ask for advice. What you need are questions, questions more about your thinking than about what you may have been doing. In this case expertise is far less important than trust. You would be best to develop a cadre of people you trust and who understand what you'd be looking for—not someone to solve your problem, but someone to probe your perspective and line of thinking. You might even want to develop a set of questions that your coaches can use to get your thinking process started then give them complete permission to ask anything about the way you've been thinking. Try these as possibilities:

1) What are you trying to accomplish; tell me what results you are after and what you are trying to learn.
2) Tell me how you arrived at your approach.
3) What facts have you based your approach on?
4) Was there anything you were trying to avoid in developing your approach your approach?
5) Are you the right person to be working on this issue?

These types of questions are designed to have you uncover assumptions that have been made consciously or unconsciously that may have limited the effectiveness of the actions you are taking. Remember to have them stay clear of questions like, "Have you done this?" That's a problem-solving question. When you see where you are stuck you will see what there is to do. If you don't know how to do it, then it will be up to you to find someone who does, and either have them show you how or do it for you.

One of the great pitfalls to avoid in any coaching conversation is having it lapse into a "checklist" approach; or to operate from the perspective that the only solutions that you may consider are those that you can implement alone. I cannot tell you how many coaching conversations I've been in where the person being coached could not consider a possible solution because they had self-limited to only those solutions they could implement.

In any coaching conversation the focus should always be *the result to be produced*, without concern for "who" will eventually produce it. With the result to be produced in the foreground and the freedom of knowing that getting credit, or being "the man," has no place in the conversation, it may make it a lot easier to proceed. The tricky part here is always not to reject the ideas that emerge from the questioning process; remember, you are the one who can't see how to get the job done. Keeping your attention on the Greater Good and the result to be produced will help you fend off any reactive responses to defend yourself or sidestep a question because it makes you uncomfortable. Go back to my basketball story if you need an example.

14

Coaching Others

Being ready to offer support, especially
to those who have let us down. Letting
others communicate without fear of
negative consequence for being
the messenger with the bad news

Now what about Coaching, or Being a Coach? I do not concern myself with techniques as much as the attitude of one who chooses to coach, either a co-worker or a direct report. In either case we are being offered a privilege. If there is a more precious gift than being listened to by another human being, I have not found it. Nor is there any greater penalty we can impose in a relationship than to revoke our listening to another.

> *To give up yourself without regret is the greatest*
> *charity.*
>
> Bodhidharma

As a coach we are being asked to bring our attention and concern to the momentary stuckness of another person. This is a big request, never to be taken lightly. The pressures of our society, absent life-threatening circumstances, make it difficult to justify asking for anything that might indicate that you are not a fully capable adult. I have actually heard managers I've worked with speak derisively about witnessing co-workers asking each other for assistance. "Isn't that a sign of weakness?" they ask.

As you consider accepting an invitation to coach, the first and most important thing to recognize and ground yourself in is that in our model Coach is a role that represents a non-attached perspective—it is not dependent on content expertise, it is not a position or rank. In the model we've created, Coach is a relationship to the person Being Coached, invited by them and only valid so long as they say so. If you've been invited to serve as someone's coach remember that the focus is on service, not expertise. You are not now and forever the coach, you are momentarily the coach, and as soon as the person who asked you to do this is done Being Coached, poof...you turn back into a pumpkin!

Both roles in a Coaching relationship are characterized by humility. This humility is grounded in reality, i.e., there is *something* that is not happening and there's no denying it! There is some set of stakes to be considered as well; again, it matters to someone that the something does happen. Ideally, it should matter to both parties that it's not happening; that way the investment in the conversation is likely to be greater.

Business and Life Coaching have become popular professions in recent years. There are now certifications offered following extended training. I have no reason to think that these are anything but wonderful opportunities for people both to coach and be coached in the midst of the complexity of our lives at this point in time. I also imagine that usually people in these professions are looking for long term engagements with specific objectives to be achieved. To be involved in coaching as I am distinguishing it here is not to be concerned with qualification as much as intent. The vast majority of opportunities to be invited to coach would likely be more spontaneous and momentary in nature. You may want to consider the kind of training offered through a certification program and that's fine, but I don't think it matters whether you are planning to move into that profession. The doing here is much the same, but the key variable is the desire on the part of someone else to seek support.

The request or invitation you receive is the initiation point for the relationship. I imagine the network and history you develop and the power of the relationships you have worked to develop, establishes a reputation that lets folks know you are able see that they are struggling—and without judgment extend to them an offer of support. Be clear though that all you can do is offer; until they accept, you can make no difference. I've had managers tell me in a very insistent manner that they did not agree with me on this point. Their people reported to them (the managers), therefore their people had to allow themselves to be coached! My response, as it usually is in instances like this where I step on the hoof of a sacred cow, is to simply ask, "How's that working for you?" Almost invariably I find a very frustrated manager under all the bluster who has not been at all prepared for the role he or she is in, afraid or unwilling to ask for assistance for fear of being perceived as unqualified or a poor leader.

Similarly, I have seen people generate tremendous frustration and anxiety when coaching was readily available, simply because their pride was more important to them than their performance. I remember a particular situation coaching a New Product Development Group of a large chemical company. The group was relatively new and had several projects going but no wins under their belt. They had been floundering about in an attempt to get one of their ideas commercialized and had asked for help in sorting out where they continued to bog down. During one particularly scattered meeting I noted that no matter what question I suggested they consider, or what was suggested by a fellow team member, all ideas were rejected, accompanied by really good reasons why the questions were not worth consideration, or could not work to elicit a powerful solution. Near the end of the meeting, at a point of great frustration I said to the group, "You know, if I didn't know better I would think I was working with a very successful team!" This stopped all the chatter and they asked why I had said that, and I replied, "The way you folks respond to the questions being posed would indicate that you really do know something about new product development, but the evidence is pretty clear that you don't, so maybe it is me who is confused." The mood of the meeting shifted at that point; one by one, the members of the groups acknowledged that they had more to learn. They began to do more listening, much less talking, and we moved forward to several successful commercializations within a relatively short period of time.

There is of course more to the doing of coaching than I have described thus far. Books and courses on coaching abound these days, and so, rather than make this book any longer than it needs to be, I hope you will be interested enough to reach out for more information.

As important as the present moment is your commitment to your value in the future, and here Coaching and Being Coached are powerful ways to be engaged. If you are committed to your value in the future it becomes imperative to seek out mentors or be willing to be a mentor in some cases. The rapid rate of change, driven by technology, is affecting every industry; there are no exceptions. With this fact as a background, then each of us who choose the life of standing on our own two feet will never become complacent about our skills.

I hear lots of talk about life-long learning, but when I hear it there is an almost goo-goo-eyed academic ring to it, as if we were in the midst of a discussion of the value of art in our lives. Please make no mistake about this concept:

The new economy will be very harsh with those who let their skills atrophy, and playing catch-up is not the place to come from. Don't be fooled into thinking that there is even a shred of the old loyalty conversation hanging about, and that maybe you could cash in some loyalty credits if you get a bit behind in your competence. You will try to cash those loyalty credits and they'll have the value of a Confederate Dollar the day after Appomatox.

While you are no longer going to cite loyalty as your primary reason for staying in an employment situation, there is good reason to seek out employers who are cognizant of the new deal. After all, we are speaking in terms of deals here and it will be in the best interest of any employer to participate with you in this process, once you have demonstrated value to the enterprise. Remember, you are not in this alone, and you and the likes of you are in short supply and in big demand these days.

There should be plenty of room in any current employment arrangement for provisions to further develop your competencies, including your collaborative skills. How about negotiating for a personal development budget as part of your employment package? This budget would be yours to spend each year, and you would be willing to demonstrate added competency. I believe any employer who understands the new economy would be open to such a proposal.

I can remember when numerous employers had tuition reimbursement plan for employees attending college. This was of course an artifact of the patriarchal employment relationship. There was not a lot of design to the plan and I cannot say I ever saw a real statement of return on investment. In this economy I think you can set your sights much higher than tuition reimbursement and think in terms of the type of educational/training support you will want to have available in your working environment. It is now possible, with the aid of technology, to provide everything from expert subject matter assistance in real time to opportunities to participate in speculative conversations on next stage technology applications for the purpose of planning education. There is no excuse for any employment environment not to have access to both types of educational opportunity and everything in between.

I think it will be up to you as someone standing on your own two feet, being your own agent, to be insistent to seek or create this type of working environment for yourself as well as those you work with. Though I do believe this is common sense, the barrier you run into will always be short-term economic thinking. Don't put up with it! You will pay for it in the end. Don't ever forget, it is about something much more than money (yours) and your family's welfare and all that, it is about the time of your life, the only thing you really own.

15

Where Do We Go From Here?
(Or, When Dancing with Tigers, Be Sure to Wear Your Steel-Toed Shoes!)

Thoughts on how the world could be. Musings on how it will likely be. Challenges to the reader to make the world a place that works for everyone and everything

W here do we go from here? Why hasn't Mike given us more specifics on what to do in order to develop the ability to adapt and to Thrive? How do we ground ourselves in a world without borders? And what's this about tigers?

In the programs I conduct, these are some questions I hear on the final day as we prepare to head back into a regular working schedule; all but the one about the tigers. My responses are nearly the same: Since you are now at a new beginning where would you *like* to go? It's your life, what would you like to do? As for grounding, you'll do that in your relationships with each other. That's all that's lasting, anyway. As far as the global expansion of capitalism, there is not much for any of us to do. That genie is out of the bottle and won't be going back soon. Our best personal course of action is to maintain a state of

preparation, and that means to adopt an attitude of adaptability and a preference for interdependence.

Developing a Capacity for Adaptation

*During periods of discontinuous, abrupt change,
the essence of adaptation involves a keen sensitivity
to what should be abandoned—not what should be
changed or introduced. A willingness to depart from
the familiar has distinct survival value.*

Peter Drucker

*Adaptability is not imitation. It means power of
resistance and assimilation.*

Mohandas Ghandi

*Gently eliminating all obstacles to his own
understanding, he constantly maintains his
unconditional sincerity. His humility, perseverance,
and adaptability evoke the response of the universe
and fill him with divine light.*

Lao Tzu, father of Taoism

There you have the advice of three masters, one a master
of business theory, Peter Drucker; one a master of politics
and societal change, Mohandas Ghandi; and one a master of spiritual practice, Lao Tzu. There is a connection
between what all three have to say here about adaptability which may or may not be readily apparent. Drucker
speaks of "letting go," Ghandi to "resistance," and Lao
Tzu to "humility and perseverance." These are perhaps not
immediately connectable unless you can hear what's in the
background of the comments. I hear *constancy of purpose* as
the melody behind the lyrics in all three songs.

Each of these teachers focused on different aspects of
human endeavor and concerns. To make their points each

utilized a vocabulary rich in the concepts of the concerns they addressed. Each shows us the world through a particular set of lenses, yet we must make no mistake, it is all the same world. Often our thinking about the world and about reality gets separated into compartments. The truth is, there is only one world and many ways of speaking about it. Throughout the course of this book I have done as much as I could to establish the validity and connection between the business, political and spiritual ways of thinking about reality. I think it unfortunate that we allow ourselves the convenience of compartmentalization, because it often legitimizes separations that are only fictions of speech, and provides opportunity to diminish one or more of these domains of perceiving reality.

Take for instance the phrase commonly invoked when business decisions with unequal economic impact on people are made: "It's just business, it's not personal." The only thing not personal about these decisions is that they were not made as a way to "get someone,"—unless they are—but they do of course always "get someone," whether intentionally or otherwise. When it's your position that's eliminated it's pretty hard not to see the action as political, or to remember that it's not personal, when it has a directly personal consequence to you and your personal business concerns, and maybe your life. Compartmentalization renders us sightless to what is important but perhaps not urgent, and therefore weakens our ability to deal with the changes affecting our futures, except as frantic reactions or bitter complaints about the unfairness of life. We do not really have work lives and personal lives. We have *lives*, and the choices we make about where we choose to spend our time.

The Practice of Adaptation

The first step in developing the capacity for adaptation may be recognizing the fact of having only one life, filled with the possibility of choices. Seeing work life and personal life as two separate worlds is a convenient compartmentalization for having sold out on the idea of our purpose in life. No wonder getting laid off or having our position outsourced is so devastating spiritually and emotionally, as well as psychologically. Having already sold out on having or following a life purpose, we are now faced with the ultimate insult: "Hey, remember that deal you made where you traded your own self-expression for a paycheck; well, it's null and void!" I wouldn't wish that on anyone.

How successful each of us will be in our approaches to the future has a lot to do with the views Drucker, Ghandi and Lao Tzu have provided us about the place adaptation plays in our lives. If we have a purpose that we have created and invested in, the continued expression of this purpose will actively inform our choices and provide a path for adaptation.

My own case in point: In the weeks and months following the events of September 11, 2001, it became increasingly apparent that many of the clients we were doing business with had been hit hard by the economic fallout, and would not be able to continue our relationship into the following year, in spite of the good work we were doing. We made efforts to generate new relationships or rekindle old accounts, to no avail.

By the beginning of the year-end holiday season it became obvious that we were not going to be able to remain at the same level of employment we had at the start of the year. We had thirteen employees at the time and by my calculations we had enough business in our pipeline to keep about three of us occupied. This was a situation I had never had to face before, and as the majority owner of the business it was going to be up to me to initiate the next course of action. Historically, I had made very few decisions by myself, preferring to involve members of the staff. To me this was one time I should not move ahead alone.

I convened a group of the employees that had worked with me the longest and asked them to help me make the best decision for the business and for the people who worked there. If you had asked me to list the ten topics I'd most like to address during the holidays, this conversation wouldn't have made the list. Some of the people who worked with me had been around for virtually the entire lifetime of our business—a lot of years. After several hours' deliberation we agreed to a course of action that involved releasing everyone from our employ by March 31st of 2002, three months away. It was our hope that although this was a short time it would give people a running start on the next steps for themselves, and we would set up schedules so folks could spend whatever time was needed to find another engagement for themselves. We mainly used our credit line to cover salaries and did our best to watch out for each other in the intervening three months. I spent a good portion of the final days of the holiday season meeting with the people who worked with me one-on-one to let them know of the decision, and to ask their partnership as we did what we could to regenerate, while at the same time approaching the situation with eyes wide open.

Eventually all but four people left. I am happy to say that almost all of those who left have fared well in the intervening period. One thing crisis does is crystallize thinking that may have been murky for a while. Three of the people who left began their own practices and we use one of them in our work now as additional support when the occasions arise. One chose to move to another firm similar to ours. We see her regularly for lunch and are following her first pregnancy with great interest. One we have since asked to rejoin us, and she remains with us now and we hope will never leave. Another moved to Florida, moved back, found a position in New York City that allowed her to live in Rochester, lived with my wife and me for two years and just bought our house, as we are moving west to be closer to our granddaughter. I wish I could say that everything turned out for everyone but it didn't. In one case we parted company under less than ideal conditions and have not been successful in repairing that relationship to this day.

It took us nearly a year to build ourselves back to a fully functional business. We adapted to our circumstances and, guided by our purpose, made our way successfully to the next chapters in our lives.

Regardless of what had happened next I was already going somewhere; it's the same somewhere I have been going for the past twenty-five years, on my way to offer what I can to show others how to reduce the suffering in their own work experience. If I look at the *circumstances* over the past nineteen years I might say I'd made little progress. If I look back at the *experience* I can say I have come a long way. If I look forward I can see there is plenty of future left, more than enough to keep me busy for many years to come.

So I am satisfied. I am already where I am going. For me it's just a matter of who am I going to meet along my path this week? Here is a point for you to consider. I am satisfied with having arrived some time ago at where I am going with my life, and I am not finished; not finished by a long shot. I am satisfied because I have found the work of my lifetime in what I am doing now. I found it by listening to myself for the path that I would follow—my personal dharma. My path was not obvious from my history or my education. Strangely enough, I found my path by trusting my interests instead of my "shoulds." I believed that if I had truly found my calling then satisfaction would be my reward. If not, my experience would tell me to look elsewhere. I believe this is the process and the reward for anyone who seeks and follows their dharma. Let me quickly add that having found my path does not make my life problem-free. I still have my children to raise, my bills to pay, my issues with health, I need to watch what I eat, get enough exercise, etc.

So, then, what is the difference? For me it is mainly in the experience of dealing with all these things. These things are the stuff of life; my path is the context in which the stuff is resolved. Somehow engaging the stuff of my life in a context I have chosen makes them all seem right, like, "Of course, what else would I be doing?" I make this statement to the people in my programs and they grimace and ask, "How could that be? It requires a faith that does not seem affordable."

I have no easy answer to this question, except to say that when you become determined to rid yourself of every notion or belief about what your life should look like in favor of what you want your life to *be* like, it seems to become an easier task. This kind of approach to life might look to others like a lot of "giving up" because it winds up with you not necessarily wanting what you *should* want, according to society; and then you may feel self-conscious. I do think that one of the great myths we'd all best confront right here is whether anyone but you, and maybe your parents or your family, really cares what your life looks like. I'm willing to bet that in our culture, where people are so busy with the process of *having*, if you get focused on *being* they won't even notice. If you do decide to focus on being, depending on the neighborhood you live in, it's probably a still a good idea to keep your lawn looking neat, but that's about it. You don't want to draw too much of the wrong kind of attention. Unfortunately, a great mistake people make is that as they attempt to find their own path they reject or disrespect the patterns left behind. There is no real freedom in this approach. And by the way, a focus on being does not rule out having; in fact it may end up making more sense and be even more enjoyable.

Satisfaction and Ambition

I've found that there are common disabling themes among my clients and the people who work with and for them. Among them is one I consider more insidious than all the rest: the notion that satisfaction is the enemy of ambition. I've actually had very, very accomplished clients tell me that they are afraid to be satisfied. They fear that satisfaction will render them ineffective and vulnerable in this highly competitive society. I do not think they understand the difference between satisfaction and complacency.

I find myself at exactly the opposite place from complacent. I live in a state of high alert. These days I am less concerned economically than I am politically. I have for 59 years fared just fine economically and have no reason to think that in the future I will do otherwise. On the other hand, I am not as certain about large portions of our population that have never experienced any period of either hard times or failures to succeed, as we move into an ever more uncertain future. I've been broke, a couple of times; I've been out of business. "Most people" have neither been broke, really broke, nor been out of business, and they probably believe they might not recover if either ever happened for them. They are wrong, because both broke and out of business are *experiences* as well as circumstances.

When people are paralyzed by the fear of a circumstance you can't really tell them that for the most part those are just periods of inconvenience, anymore than you can tell someone what the Sistine Chapel or the Taj Mahal or even Disney World are really like if they haven't been there. Try telling someone what being broke was like as an experience, in an attempt to take the edge off the circumstance; it doesn't work. I tried asking my friends to imagine being back in college on a Friday night deciding whether to eat or buy beer—or putting our stereos up on planks and cinder blocks because real shelves would be too expensive. Not the most dire example, I know, but a familiar feeling for a lot of us. My friends did not find even these to be comforting images to consider. I tried telling them that it's mainly inconvenient until you get things rolling again, but they just knew it would be tragic; not so much for what it was as what it meant: It meant you had failed; no, more precisely, You are a failure! We can hear all the stories about how Abraham Lincoln failed so many times before he was elected President, and it still does not remove the fear of the stigma of failure.

I ran into a friend of mine shortly after the severe business downturns that affected many of us after both the dot-com bust and the September 11 tragedies. She had heard that our business had taken a downturn. If you can call losing 90% of your revenue sources in one quarter a downturn, I suppose she was correct! I've already given you most of the details of these events. We had to release virtually our entire staff and basically reboot the business. She asked cautiously how I was doing. I responded by asking her if she wanted to know how I was doing, which was great, or how "things" were? She laughed and said that of all the people she knew, I was probably the only one who would make that distinction. She said she wanted to know about both. I told her that I was great and things were difficult at the moment. If there is nothing you take from what you have read here please take this: **The notion of a path in life has nothing to do with the material circumstances.**

Your path is a spiritual and experiential matter. If you continue to look in the material realm for your path you will likely be disappointed. If you do find your path you are not guaranteed success in matters material. This is not a negotiation! It is also not a matter of choosing one over the other. In this life both the material and the spiritual are realms to be responsible for. We have an opportunity to fail in both realms. Being broke or out of business is only about not having money; it does not exclude a rich experience of

satisfaction. Being materially successful does not guarantee any sense of satisfaction. Being impoverished means no
money, no sense of self-satisfaction and no opportunity for
either. I've never been impoverished, nor do I expect to be.
That would be tough to get over.

A Concern for the Political in Life

Now as I said earlier, politically I am concerned; that's
an altogether different set of questions. I do not limit my
discussion of politics to affairs of government. My concerns
and attention have more to do with any situation where
unhealthy self-interest overrides interdependency; where
power gets out of balance and people trade their self-
expression for a paycheck; where employers use threats
instead of inspiration and collaborative offers. What I mean
by unhealthy self-interest is no apparent recognition or
regard for the future, approaching life purely on a trans-
actional basis, doing whatever you must to get what you
want now. A very costly way to live life, for you and for
those you encounter.

Politics requires participation in the pursuit of a
particular set of interests. This fact of life is often very
challenging, not so much for myself, but certainly for the
people I interact with, many of whom have not a clue
about their own path or even its existence. I am very clear
that we live in a time and a set of circumstances that must
be considered broadly, and which left misunderstood could
lead to grave personal and social consequences. As we
advance towards a fully global economy we are indeed
"dancing with tigers." (So I finally worked in the tigers.)
They are obviously metaphorical tigers. My tigers stand
for the ultimate product of capitalism collaborating with
globalization: the multinational corporation.

I have no bone to pick with the multinational corporation. Neither do I necessarily object to nuclear power.
How do I connect these two thoughts? To me both mul-

tinational corporations and nuclear power are cut from the same cloth, both very real opportunities, both possibly very beneficial, both possibly devastating when used without caution or conscience. As we continue to support the internationalization of our corporations we are introducing a feature into our lives that while graceful, powerful and beautiful is dangerous as well—like dancing with tigers. And we love to see the tigers dance; we pay money for the thrill.

When in the midst of our entertainment the tiger does what tigers do, steps on our toe, or worse, we pull back in horror and ask, "How could that have happened? Bad tiger!" We may have already begun asking that question and we shake our heads as we read stories of fellow citizens being displaced by global outsourcing. We'll be even keener about the issue when the tiger steps on our own toe!

So, does this mean we should close our borders and raise our import tariffs? I would not favor action like that any more than I would favor the cessation of the use of nuclear power for peaceful purposes. Buckminster Fuller often warned of the dangers of nuclear power. He did not believe that as a species we could be trusted with such an instrument and not use it for purposes detrimental to humanity in general, even just for purposes of power generation. I feel much the same with the expansion of multinational corporations. Are we mature enough to conduct ourselves with the interest of the many in the foreground? I am not certain. I do believe that the enemy is not the system, the system is neutral. It seems to me that what is occurring is the natural expression of a capitalist system on a global level, for the very first time in history.

What may not be so natural is the method of expression, the public corporation. The corporate structure has allowed for unprecedented economic progress and development of wealth. It has at the same time allowed for unprecedented lack of social responsibility, because with the separation of ownership from management we have truly allowed the advancement of capitalism without conscience. It's a potentially dangerous thing when left without the kind of oversight that demands responsibility to the larger public interest.

Unfortunately, it may ultimately be that the greatest danger to our free society is the unfettered expansion of multinational corporations and the economic destabilization that can result. And would that not be ironic if it were to be that we were mauled by our own pet tiger?

16

The Politics of Interdependence

Facing the challenge of living in a "political reality," as we always will

If from this book you have been influenced in some way to consider choosing a path of interdependence, there are some things I want you to consider and be aware of— namely, the *politics* of interdependence. Yes, that's what I said, interdependence has its political aspects too!

There is a phrase I hear in business a lot, and it is graphic and represents this message well. The phrase is, "to throw someone under the bus." If you haven't heard and understood that one, its meaning will become clear. In the times we spend at work there are occasions when we perceive a threat to our identity, position, or personal economic security. We're tempted to want someone other than ourselves to be spotlighted in these situations, so we may try to refocus attention towards another party. We ask that someone else be in the path of accountability; hence the metaphor of the bus. It's the kind of instinctual survival behavior from when we were kids and our older brother or sister shifted blame for some transgression from them to us in the presence of our parents' disapproval, or we did it to a younger sibling.

Chances are good that almost all of us at one point or another in our adult working career have been in a situation where shifting blame seemed like a good idea; like a gut reaction, not a carefully thought out response. If you have, I am hoping that you can recall it in detail and the experience that followed. These are life and death occasions as far as I am concerned, life and death for your soul, your integrity, your sense of Self.

Life and death sounds dramatic, but I'm using the term intentionally to underscore that there are forms of death other than physical. Death of the spirit or soul can happen at any time in our lives. Once we sell out our fellow man in favor of our own survival we are faced with options (we have already made a choice). One option is to own what we have done, fully experience the consequences of our action, apologize for damage done and allow the event to teach us about how we want to live. Another option, one taken quite often, is to justify our choice and not hold ourselves to account. When taken, this option begins the process of the death of the soul and there is never a guarantee that we will turn it around.

How is this political, you ask? First, I do not think of politics as a bad or evil thing, that is unfortunate baggage. Consider this definition from my Merriam-Webster Unabridged Dictionary:

> **Politics,** *noun,* competition between competing interest groups or individuals for power and leadership.

Given the diversity of views among people, given the diversity of interests in any organization, what would ever make us think that we would have anything other than politics? Basically, when two or more people get together for any reason you have a political situation.

We have differences of opinion, we have differences

in desires and we do our best to influence each other to our way of seeing or doing things. That's politics, that's human interaction, that's normal—and we'd do ourselves a favor by making peace with the reality of politics. To think otherwise is to invite suffering. In our resistance to politics, make no mistake, there is suffering. You may be most familiar with the effects of resistance to politics: the cynical attitudes toward things political and the frequently accompanying presence of cynicism towards life in general.

Now this is where the "dancing tigers" may do us in. From a political perspective I am not confident that when push comes to shove and times get tougher (and you should count on it coming to this), if we have done little or nothing to preserve our freedoms they will suddenly seem very, very precious. And here I'm talking about civil as well as economic freedoms.

Voltaire, the French philosopher of the 18th century, offered an insightful thought as regards the relationship between money and religion: *When it is a question of money, everybody is of the same religion.* Inasmuch as I am familiar with Voltaire's intent when he uttered these words he might also have said, "When it is a question of money everybody is a citizen of the same nation."

Is there a choice then around politics? I say no, because there will always be politics. Where choice does exist is in whether we are all clear about the game we are playing. Many of us are not clear, and there is a consequence to remaining unclear. Without clarity of purpose politics of any sort may well look like a personal threat rather than the normal process of human interaction. Without a doubt I say that the single most certain foes of satisfaction and interdependence are either not knowing what you want or settling for less than what you want.

Consider that going to a restaurant could become a political event. You may think this is a stretch. The stakes (ouch!) are not so high in this game, your money and satisfaction for one transaction, and their convenience and profitability, but all the same there is a game afoot. Here's the game: The restaurant does not offer an unlimited menu. Generally, the menu is fixed. The idea is to provide a broad enough set of offerings to satisfy "most people," not all people. The fixed menu allows the management the chance of doing a good job of ordering supplies, controlling portions and making a profit. An unlimited menu would be unmanageable and probably unprofitable, a constant guessing game. The elements of satisfaction and interdependence are, I hope, obvious here.

How you play the game: You are interested in a satisfying meal at a decent price. Sometimes the event is more social than this but let's go with this for the moment. You arrive; you are seated and presented with a menu. You have chosen this place because its reputation is stellar. In looking over the menu you notice several items that have an appeal and yet there are none that combine the entrée with the side dish you prefer. Rats! So what do you want? Do you want the pork chop with garlic mashed potatoes or with rice pilaf and spiced apples, as is offered? If this is a purely social occasion it may not matter to you but that's not what we are discussing here. This is an issue of personal satisfaction. This is the moment of truth. Will you "settle" for the pork chop with rice and apples, a nice meal and not exactly what you want? Or will you address the dilemma? Will you ask for what you want? I know this sounds silly, but you have no idea how many people will not ask, will not speak up, will settle for less than they want and pay for less than they want. It's a staggering number, probably consistent with the 70%+ people at work that the Gallup organization has determined are disengaged in their current occupation.

Every day I deal with people in the workplace who have never had a thought of asking for what they want. They have gotten used to pork chops with rice and apples.

It's not a bad meal, it's just not what they want, consequently not satisfying. Within broad limits the restaurant has a commitment to our satisfaction, this choice is essential to the nature of the interdependency. But satisfaction has no absolute value; it's a product of the experience of the exchange taking place. The restaurant gets what it wants by seeing to it that we get what we want. That has not been the nature of "employment" for as long as any of us can remember. I think we need to face the fact that while our places of employment are not exactly like restaurants they are political environments, they are interdependent relationships and there is power at stake, (ouch again).

In most restaurants when you ask for something different than what you see on the menu they do their best to respond to your request. They are, after all, competing for your business. Truth is, as much as employers say that people are their most important asset they frequently do not act like it. Primarily and pragmatically, employers are interested in their business and not in what employees want. Most employers are not even interested in getting the best their employees have to offer. They settle too, they settle for employees doing only what they're are asked to do. This constitutes a conspiracy of silence in which all parties are culprits. We have never really seen the best from either our businesses or their employees. Can this be changed, can we create working environments that ask for and reward the best that people have to give? I believe so, but it's not predictable; it's not predictable unless there is a paradigm shift.

I see nothing about the present or future economic situation that will prompt employers to call forth the shift I am suggesting. The paradigm of the employer remains immediate and profoundly pragmatic, and what I am looking at is far from immediately pragmatic, though I think it ultimately *is* pragmatic. There is a leap of faith required that will be far easier for the individual to make than an organization, especially if it happens to be publicly traded.

What might working environments be like if there were to be a paradigm shift? To what would we shift? I've asked that question many times in my workshops. We start by listing the elements of a traditional employment paradigm—the one most of us find ourselves in today—and then I ask people to invent another possible way of being related, beyond simply employer-to-employee. Here's a sample of what folks have come up with:

Traditional Employment Paradigm

Mode of participation: Compliance
Based on? The employed needing the employment
Relationship: Top down
Talents: Bring only the talents you are asked for
Primary connection: Financial security
Focus: A job
Responsibility: Only for your part
Identify with: Self concerns
Approach to problems: Identify and point out only

The picture here is one in which the employee has limited initiative and a limited role in the enterprise—a sad but true profile we're all too familiar with.

For the new paradigm of relationship these categories take on a whole new energy. Again and again, the "wish lists" in my workshops make the same points—based on a paradigm of **Partnership**.

Partnership Paradigm

Mode of participation: Engagement
Based on? Freely chosen partnership

Relationship: Democratic
Talents: Bring all you have
Primary connection: Emotional investment
Focus: A career
Responsibility: To the whole business
Identify with: Community concerns
Approach to problems: Identify and offer solutions

Admittedly, I was the one who suggested the term Partnership, and people in the workshops had misgivings. However, when we defined Partnership outside the limited definitions normally associated with the term, equal share, equal voice, etc. and considered an environment focused on equality of value to all parties, we arrived at these criteria.

Would the environment described by the second set of criteria be attractive to you? That's not a rhetorical question, as I have found that there are people, though not as many as in years gone by, who if given the option would choose the traditional employment environment. Today, I do not believe that is "most people."

If I am right or even close, in assuming that my understanding of most people is that they would prefer the Partnership paradigm, then another question immediately follows: Would you be willing to do whatever is needed to create an environment like this for yourself? Again, this is not a rhetorical question. I am not saying that you should do anything, but if there is an appeal to operating in this manner I ask you to consider this: For all we know—and never mind beliefs for the moment—this is it for us, this lifetime. No matter how careful we are or how successful we are, how many risks we take or how many times we may fail, this lifetime ends up exactly the same for each of us. The opportunity we have to make a difference for ourselves and those around us is to face this reality, not as fatalistic but as definite. What we have each been given in varying amounts is the time of our lives. It is our choice how we decide to live it, it is our choice where and with whom we decide to spend it. For myself I have chosen to spend it doing something I love doing, with people I enjoy doing it with, and I'll do it for as long as it is truly what I want and not a day longer.

I invite you to take the same approach. I do not expect you to take on the fate of humanity; there is no need for that. I would encourage you to take on the world you influence and work in, that one right around you, where you can have a say in how things go. I am confident that if most people do this it will produce a world that I'll be glad I lived in, and so will you.

I am quite sure that if enough of us take this approach alongside each other, that eventually our paths will cross. And when they do, I'll be prepared to offer my best to support your purpose, and I will be very surprised if I am not rewarded in kind.

17

Afterword to Employers

Attracting (and keeping) the people you really need

The first job of a leader is to define reality. The last is to say thank you. In between the two, the leader must become a servant and a debtor.

Max DuPree, *Leadership is an Art*

Recently, I was sitting across the table from a new client, senior manager of a very successful home products company. I had just finished reading Friedman's *The World is Flat*, and asked whether he had seen it. He hadn't and asked what it was about. I told him that it had really opened my eyes to something I had begun to suspect a couple of years ago. After I gave him a few of the anecdotal references, he said, "Sounds interesting, but I know you, Mike, you wouldn't be bringing this up if you didn't have a point to make."

"Not so much a point," I replied, "more of a question. I've been wondering about something for a while, about your company, and reading the book just reminded me of how much I wanted to ask this."

"So let's hear it," he said.

"The catalog services group of your business has been growing steadily for several years and it looks like the biggest growth may still be in front of you. But you don't seem to be making much use of technology as you are growing. You're adding more employees rather than investing in technology solutions, like perhaps making more use of the Internet."

He agreed, saying, "Yes, we've added a lot of people. We know we ought to eventually be considering technology solutions but we've always been a 'high touch' company for our customers, and so far we are hitting our numbers without going away from that strategy and making the big investments in technology. We're just waiting until the right time to apply more technology. But what's your question?"

"My question is this: Has it ever crossed your mind that the work that's being done in that area is not especially high skilled and doesn't call for a background understanding of business or even the technical aspects of home products for that matter? Most of the people I meet out there are reasonably educated, most with bachelor's degrees, but what they are doing doesn't require a college education; in fact, the skills associated with what they are doing are mainly acquired on the job."

Now he seemed a bit frustrated, "Yes, sure…it probably doesn't take a college degree in finance or even a college degree at all to fill those positions. Many of those people do have degrees but they are not necessarily business degrees; they are liberal arts degrees like English or Philosophy, or social science degrees like Sociology. We hire these people quite frankly because we have a plentiful supply in our local area, since they don't have that many employment choices. For many of them this is their hometown, and they would like to stay. They also tend to be better communicators and a bit more mature than the average high school graduate that doesn't go on to college. Our customer service is important to us. That sort of goes with the 'high touch' approach, right?"

"Well," I said, carefully bypassing his bid for my agreement, "that's kind of what I thought. I was also wondering if you had considered that other countries where English is well spoken have a plentiful supply of college graduates. They are also well educated, good communicators and have a desire to stay in the areas where they were born. I'll bet there are a lot of those folks who could pick up the necessary skills quite easily, and they are a lot less expensive than what you are paying the folks in your customer response center." My client began to fidget a bit in his chair.

"But I want to keep these jobs local," he blurted, "wouldn't just about anyone? And besides, we are making our numbers doing what we are doing now."

"So, you're keeping the jobs here for the community, like a public service?" I said. "I do agree that almost anyone would want to keep the jobs local, but you are not just anyone. I was of the impression that as a senior manager and an officer in a public company you had an obligation to act in the best interest of the investors, the stock holders—many of whom in this case are also employees of the company."

"That's right, and that's what I believe we are doing. We're following the strategy that got us to this point; it seems to continue to work."

"Doesn't it sort of depend on how you define 'working'? I know you are making your numbers but hasn't your stock been flat for some time now? I think if I were in your shoes I might be feeling somewhat vulnerable, at least in my role as an officer. What if one of your competitors has a major breakthrough in their cost structure? Where does that leave you?"

Again he fidgeted, "Well we are already having many

of our products made outside the U.S. I'm not all that comfortable with that approach, but we've had to do that just to keep our prices even with the competition. I hesitate to think about using service providers from outside the country, too. Then about the only thing about us that would be American would be our certificates of incorporation. I am not sure our customers or our shareholders would go for that."

I knew we were near the end of the time we had allocated for our meeting, but I decided to go ahead and open another vein. "What about your employees? Do they have any idea how vulnerable they are?"

"I can't be responsible for them in that way," said my client. "It seems like you are going too far with this conversation and I am not sure I like the obligation you may be inferring."

There would not be time that day to complete the conversation so I quickly assured him, "Please don't think I am inferring anything. I am just asking the question because I think before long you will need to ask it. Now you have the luxury of just knowing it is there to be considered. We can pick this up some other time. I just wanted to get you thinking about the new reality."

He looked at me with a wry smile. "OK then, you accomplished what you had in mind. I'll be thinking about this for the rest of the week."

Does this story seem far-fetched? I imagine not, nor should it. For several years now employment opportunities have been moving to locations around the world where there is at least equal competence, sometimes better, and the cost of doing business is significantly less. What's new is that now the migration of opportunity is rapidly moving upstream. In many ways we here in America helped with our liberal immigration policies. Where language was a barrier, that has diminished; much of the world has developed an English speaking capability along with new educational capabilities in a carefully designed effort to become part of the global economy. And now most dramatically, as a result of technology, distance is no longer a barrier to participation. The "world" of business is awake 24 hours a day, 365 days a year.

I have enormous compassion for my client. I do not envy in many ways the decisions that lie in front of him and his counterparts, whether in this company or any other. Is there a right thing to do? I don't necessarily think there is. Yet, without restructuring the way we consider the question there is only one predictable outcome. I do think there is a justifiable thing to do: outsource, which is made right by the beliefs of the capitalist system of thinking. The irony that may not be obvious at the moment is that this very system, capitalism, has given us the challenges our leadership must now face. And it is the limitations of the capitalist way of thinking that will blind us to possible solutions.

Before you think I am going to suggest revolution, hold back. I am going to suggest *evolution*, and in this case an evolution in consciousness that is creative rather than reactive. In this section I mean to illuminate a path forward without the handy justification of "capitalism doing what it was designed to do."

Albert Einstein, who has given us all so much, has also given us this:

> We can't solve problems by using the same kind of thinking we used when we created them.

I realize the theme of this book is directed to the individuals I refer to as "most people;" however, this Afterword is as important to me as the rest of the book combined. In my business I am not engaged by "most people." It is the employers of "most people" who fund my life, and it is with greatest appreciation that I share my thoughts with the employers now.

World economics have and will continue to change dramatically. I am confident that no one can say when exactly the next "steady state" will be reached. The nature of what we refer to as "work" itself has changed dramatically and the roles of the players have changed as well. But what about the most fundamental element of the equation called "being at work," the relationship between employed and employer? This relationship appears to me to be largely the same as it has been for as far back as anyone can imagine. Until this most fundamental of elements in the economic equation is changed it will be difficult to imagine, much less craft, solutions that will accommodate the forces at play on a global basis, and also foster the stability of engagement that will continue to be a foundational element of democratic societies.

There has always been a dharmic path to follow. Likely it would be most easily defined as Interdependence. To surrender to this dharmic path has never been as critical to the future as it is now. Certainly it has not always been sought, and still today seeking the dharmic approach will be a matter of choice.

All know the way, but few actually walk it.
Bodhidharma

In what follows I am going to share some thoughts on a new context for the relationships between those who would pay for assistance in their commercial enterprise and those who would accept pay for doing so. I do not limit myself here to thinking of "pay" only in monetary terms. Pay could also have to do with the overall conditions of the relationship.

Peter Drucker offers the following as guideposts to those of us who have recognized the new world and are seeking to understand the new rules of the workplace:

The historic shift to "self-management" offers organizations four basic ways to develop and motivate knowledge workers:
- *Know people's strengths*
- *Place them where they can make the greatest contributions*
- *Treat them as associates*
- *Expose them to challenges*

Peter Drucker, "Managing Knowledge Means Managing Oneself," *Leader to Leader,* Spring 2000

If you have read the previous chapters you will probably note that these words from Mr. Drucker pretty much capture the essence of what I have been recommending that "most people" look for in a working environment. If yours can be the kind of workplace these people will be looking for, you have a distinct competitive advantage. To not operate in this manner is to do so at great peril to your own interest and certainly to the interest of those in your employ. The new rules will have no mercy.

There has once again been a paradigm shift. A paradigm shift is unlike any other phenomenon in life. With an earthquake or a hurricane there is immediate evidence that something has happened, things are different and you don't have to look hard to discover that fact. Yet with all the change brought on by one of these events, things are really still the same. With any of these events in the natural world, things may well go back to being much like they were. Not so with a shift in a paradigm; once it occurs there is no going back. Things may actually, and usually do, look the same for a while and they most likely will for a while, but the rules, meanings, and pattern of understanding are all very different.

Aftermath: *noun*, the period of time following a usually ruinous event.

The aftermath of a hurricane or earthquake is only temporary. Certainly a major event took place but the rules of life have not been altered; in fact they have been exercised and adapted to. When a paradigm shifts there is a wake as its aftermath.

Wake: *noun, obs.*, the state of wakefulness; a waking up, as from sleep

Not a wake like the wake from a boat which eventually passes. Not a wake like a vigil for a deceased friend or family member before burial. No, a "wake," a period of awakening, a rousing from the slumber induced by the previous paradigm. This wake may and will likely continue for years, in some case decades. How long will it take for the wake to complete itself? It is difficult to predict. As employers you can resolve your own awakening and play an active role in awakening those you work with and those in your employ. How do you accomplish your own awakening? By accepting one fundamental element of the dharma of all life and existence on our planet, the principle of Interdependence.

Interdependence: *noun*, mutually dependent, a reciprocal relationship.

I was concerned about using the term in the context we have traditionally referred to as "employment." Initially my concern arose from the aversion I often hear expressed in the American business culture around anything suggesting "equity of reward." I thought that might interfere with some readers' ability or willingness to stay focused on my intent at this point.

All previous paradigms of economic consciousness have to one degree or another misrepresented, misunderstood or denied the fact of "interdependence." Capital and ownership have been granted an advantage in most theories or systems of economic thinking with which I am familiar. Not being an economist I am clearly out of my element here, but would I be far off if I asserted that all previous employment models have reflected relationships of unequals? Capital has historically been considered the favored or scarce resource and ownership with its inherent control of capital and assumption of ultimate risk was assumed to be the superior position in the relationship.

Secondly, I was concerned that the word "interdependence" might bear the psychological baggage of being associated with shared need or co-dependence. Neither of these concerns would represent valid interpretations of my intent.

We are here on this planet subject to its fundamental laws. And yet, the history of humanity is rife with mankind, or at least men, attempting to defy this law and declare themselves above that which applies to every other creature on the planet. To what do we ascribe this behavior? Perhaps it is our nature as humans to be arrogant.

There is also something in human nature that often promotes suffering. It is hard to imagine a more malicious plot than to establish a cultural norm that measures success in terms of material achievement. By the fundamental assumption of this standard, "more is always better," we establish a standard that can never be met and then punish ourselves for not meeting it. Camus' Sisyphus may have had a better deal; at least his rock stayed the same size all the time!

The beginnings of our own nation have in many ways laid the foundation for the shift we are now experiencing. If we could say that every shift in understanding has its own wake, then perhaps the ultimate wake of the Declaration of Independence is the awakening to Interdependence.

*In the progress of personality, first comes a
declaration of independence, then recognition of
interdependence.*

Henry Van Dyke

Many things still look the same, many others are rapidly looking different, no doubt faster than with any prior
paradigm shift experienced by humanity—and everything
in our lives will be affected.

What was occurring in the world of work in the
middle to late 80's and into the early 90's (re-engineering)
would have been similar to an earthquake had not the
breakthroughs occurred in information technology. People
were in fact being laid off in record numbers, there was
most likely going to be a downturn in the economy and
things were going to be very different than they are now.
Then the breakthroughs in technology gained momentum
and have continued, and we went from an economy where
the many were dependent on the few for employment
opportunities to one where the source of opportunity is
no longer scarce capital but abundant information—and
things will never be the same...again.

I suppose it would be possible to get into a chicken
and egg conversation regarding the emergence of the global
marketplace and advancements in information technology,
but I am pretty sure that won't change what has happened.
For me the cause-and-effect issue is handled by thinking in
terms of "happy accident."

The fundamental message of this chapter will come
down to the need we all have as employers to develop
a **radically** new relationship to the people we choose to
invite to join us in our enterprises. The term **radical** is often
one we respond to with concern, especially when used in
the context of politics. In the business context I mean it to
be somewhat political insofar as the basis of relationships
in the workplace must change, and we as employers (yes,

remember, I am one as well) are playing catch-up.

In the past, the way we went to the marketplace for human assistance might be captured in this question: "We need to have this done, can you do this?" When the mindset was that opportunity was regulated by those who controlled capital—historically owners and (since the popularization of the public corporation) professional management—the majority of people associated with an enterprise were considered "resources" to be used in the production of more capital. In the days when manual or repetitive labor was the main human resource being sought this made sense to virtually everyone. In that scenario we placed people into "jobs" which were a bundle of tasks and we expected people to do them, without regard to whether they had all the requisite talents or not.

We did not ask people what they could do; we asked them if they could do what we needed done. The people who came to us or were associated with us did not expect to be asked what they *could* do, they expected to be told what to do. This was in fact an exchange of value which favored ownership or leadership of the organization over the individual. We employed mainly on the basis of an individual having the minimal skill set or some demonstrated ability to learn that skill set. We did not employ the whole person!

I know that this makes more sense to us now but I still do not believe we have shifted far enough. If we were to relate to those we pay, in some fashion, as *assets* rather than *expenses* we might find ourselves asking different questions of these people, and taking different actions towards them. This is the *radical* shift I am recommending.

Radical: *adjective,* of or relating to the root.

As business owners or professional managers we have no one to blame for the changes we need to make, other than the Founding Fathers of this nation, or perhaps the nature of life on the planet. When the Founding Fathers created the Declaration of Independence they likely had in mind primarily the opportunity for self-government. It is commonly understood that they borrowed heavily from the Native Americans, especially the Iroquois Nation, in crafting the words and ideas of the document. Perhaps unknowingly, or maybe quite the contrary in doing so, they were taking basic principles from peoples who lived very much in collaboration or interdependence with their world.

As a nation of people we have fought for and nurtured democratic principles around the world. This effort has involved employers and employees alike. In spite of our differences we have fought to keep ourselves free. We have also involved ourselves, intentionally or not, in a process that is yet to fully unfold. While we have fought for and emphasized a democratic form of government we have not appreciated that *democratic* principles themselves are not limited to politics. The principles of democracy infer a far greater promise than political freedom.

Democratic: *adjective,* favoring or disposed to favor social equality; disregarding or overcoming class distinctions.

The full promise of living a democratic reality holds the possibility of allowing us as employers, along with those in our employ, to make a dharmic adjustment and embrace the interdependent nature of co-existence. I say this is a truth that we have known in our hearts forever. It is only our fear of interdependence, and the inherent vulnerability it brings, that keeps us from living this ideal.

There is no such thing as a "self-made" man. We are made up of thousands of others. Everyone who has ever done a kind deed for us, or spoken one word of encouragement to us, has entered into the make-up of our character and of our thoughts, as well as our success.
George Matthew Adams, 20th century philosopher

Seeing the employee as an asset will precede relating to him differently. In business we "see" through the language of finance, and "employees as assets" is going to require a different kind of accounting, a different relationship to training and development, different staffing of whatever group is responsible for the systems supporting the condition of employment—and overall, a different mindset within the management group of any organization. It is going to take Appreciating Interdependence on the part of Owners and Professional Managers. This will be as a necessary and practical—not optional—strategic shift into the new basis for the employment relationship. The Levels of Engagement that I have been urging "most people" to take on as a practice have as much application from the business to its employees as they do person-to-person. They describe a path to establish a *context* of engagement.

As an Owner or Professional Manager it seems quite possible for you to recognize the world as it is right now. I am certain that you know many employment opportunities have relocated to other parts of the world. The mood of the people you employ now is different from the mood of the past, but that is not what I am referring to. The real adjustment to the world that is needed is emotional, "a change of heart" if you will.

If you are operating a business today and have not made the shift to a much more collaborative approach, to having people work *with* you, then you are already in deep trouble. Rather than attempt to regain control of the situation, which might be our natural tendency, we must adopt a completely new approach to the relationship called "employment."

An employer can have a mindset of employees-as-resources or employees-as-assets. Notice in this chart how the nature of the business relationship changes with an employees-as-assets mindset; notice your own experience as you consider Engagement rather than Employment. Do you get excited by the possible change or does it feel somewhat threatening?

Employee as . . .		
	Resource	**Asset**
Connection	Employment	Engagement
Possibility	Compliance	Partnership
Opportunity	Security	Self-Expression
Action	Execution	Choice
Output	Money	Money + Learning

Let's call the relationship we have with people now Engagement. Let's have this term replace employment. It represents an entirely new reality, one that describes a relationship of equals intended to produce mutual benefit. Please notice that I did not say resulting in equal reward. I have spent the greater part of this book telling "most people" how to get a grip on their future. The key to the message has been to step into the world of Interdependence and begin to see things in a whole new light.

My message to employers might be put as simply as "Get Over Yourself." How did we get the idea that being the owner or the professional manager of a business was a position of royalty? This is clearly a carryover from the days of organization as the source of economic opportunity. Those days are gone, those days are gone, those days are gone!

I think it is time we told the truth so we can all get on with our lives. Maybe the time to do it is now: **As employers and professional managers we have been behaving badly for quite some time.** Someone had to say it. I do not know where we ever got the idea that when we came to work we could forget everything our mother told us about treating people the way we like to be treated and all the things we learned about sharing. I have yet to meet the person who was raised by their parents to be inconsiderate of people, or thoughtless or relate to others like they were expendable but well...this is business, and in business it is different, this is the real world after all, blah, blah, blah. I personally think we have had just about enough of this. Our businesses, our organizations can now be environments for us as employers to steward—and steward does not mean control. *The environments we will steward...*

> *Knowledge workers have become your main resource...they can leave you tomorrow. You have to make it so that they want to work with you, not for you...and we do not know how to do that.*
> Peter Drucker, *Context Magazine,* Spring 1999

Here then is another of those credible sources saying it better than I could. This from Peter Drucker is pretty much the essence of the message I want to convey to employers. The only other thing I would add, just to stress the point, is that your knowledge workers are more important to your business than your strategy. Drucker uses the term "main resource" and—I'm taking a liberty here—I wish he had said "main asset" because this would have shifted your thinking to the other side of the balance sheet.

Lest you think that I am only about the "soft stuff," let me tell you that I am not. In fact there is a strong business case for what I am about to suggest as an appropriate course of action for the employers in the modern economy.

Several years ago Bill Catlette and Richard Hadden put together a wonderful book that details some of the great success stories of companies that took or are taking an investment approach to their employees. *Contented Cows Give Better Milk* is a no-nonsense, factual look at practices that have worked and continue to work in attracting and retaining the best people for your business. In "Just the Facts," the first chapter to this useful guide, the authors offer this thought, and then back it up with data:

> *From the start, the exceptional organizations have differentiated themselves as employers of choice, thus enabling them to hire and retain top-drawer people, and then differentiated their products in the marketplace.*

When a case is as well presented as it is in *Contented Cows*, there is no sense repeating it, so I won't; but I will recommend that the book be read by Senior Managers and not just by Human Resource staffers. For some years now we have seen verbiage in corporate annual reports espousing the belief in how important the people are to the organization; I think that from a patriarchal perspective that was nice to say. It also masked the attitude that people were expenses, and to me the term "human resource," like any other resource, means something to be used, or even used up.

When the new economy took shape, the hegemony of capital as the source of opportunity quite quickly behaved as though these same "very important people" were expendable, even after years of operating as though loyalty would lead to security. Well...those days are gone, so, are those employers gone? Is that attitude gone? I can't say for sure, but I have my suspicions. It is time now to take heed of Peter Drucker's words and begin *acting* like people are the most valuable assets of any enterprise, if for no other reason than the future of your enterprise depends on it. I can wait for your heart to catch up but I don't know if your business can!

In order to accomplish this mission as an employer you might set out to create and maintain an "environment or culture of interdependence." This type of environment has little or no concern for control of human assets, but places lots of attention on systems that inform the organization of what the talent needs are, now and in the immediate future. Lots of attention is given to attracting and selecting the right people, developing them once they are on the team, and understanding the full scope of their capabilities so as to support their **adaptability** at times when the jobs they do can be moved and completed by less expensive talent.

In many ways the marketplace is already beginning to take care of the bad actors, so I am not going to ask them to repent. If you are currently building a business to sell, what I have to say may not be relevant to you anyway. Word on the bad actors is spreading faster then ever; the principle of Good Reputation holds for us as employers too. The Built to Sell folks are not so much concerned with building a "culture of development" as they are in getting big and getting out fast, so for the most part they seem to be content to "buy" their talent in hopes of cashing in before they have to learn how to relate to anybody. Now this is pure opinion on my part and I have nothing against the Built to Sell approach; it just doesn't interest me. It is a great game for those who want to play; I am, however, not a big fan of the bad actors.

Throughout this book I have been telling those who would be free to be more demanding—demanding, not in the sense of being difficult, because we all have better things to do, but refusing to settle for less than you really want. This will help employers more easily recognize those who would be partners in their working environments.

As an employer, I know that we *do*, for the most part, know the world has changed, but I believe many of us are still whimpering and relating to current events like an earthquake instead of a paradigm shift. My evidence would be that our hunger for the applications to understand our human assets does not in any way match our desire to better understand our operations. Think for a moment of the number of organizations that have invested in some form of *enterprise resource system* in the recent years. You are aware of many right off the top of your head, perhaps even your own organization. These systems, which are massive undertakings, are still not addressing the paradigm shift in the employment relationship. Yes, you will find some version of a Human Resource System as part of most of these undertakings; but for the most part these are really accounting systems for the expense of having employees, they are not true management tools. Systems for dealing with the needs of our *partners* are lagging woefully behind, if we have systems at all. There are organizations that are exceptions to be sure, and they are acting like people really are their most important asset.

I recently moved to the West Coast, but for many years I lived in New York State, where I became aware that the Wegman's Corporation was doing something right. Wegman's is a regional grocery store chain and has been named to the Top 100 Places to Work in America for several years now. A retail operation, they were rated #1 in 2005 and remain #2 in 2006. With all the excitement in other industries it might be hard to appreciate the uniqueness of this family owned business of some 70+ stores. But if you have ever been to a Wegman's store you can tell the difference in the shopping experience. Not all their stores are the same, some are still of an older design and many are in a process of upgrade and of course they have developed several of the "superstores" which combine the grocery shopping experience with the old time open market experience—and these are really fun. But my point is that no matter which of their locations you visit, you know you are shopping in a different kind of place.

I had the opportunity to visit recently with one of the people who create and deliver training to Wegman's employees. She struck me as being just as hospitable as the folks who assist me in the grocery stores. She told me that she had only very recently joined Wegman's after a long career with one of our local global companies, also considered a fine place to be employed. I asked why she had made the switch so late in her career and she said that for the last five years before leaving her other firm she had been fascinated by how Wegman's was able to get all those very young people who worked in the stores to be so pleasant, courteous and helpful. She was envious and just had to find out the secret of their customer service training. Having been at Wegman's for just over six months she said she had already learned the secret. Wegman's did in fact have fine customer service training, but now being part of the organization she said that she could see that the secret was in how they treated the people, not only how they trained them! Wegman's has been on Fortune's list of Top 100 Places to Work for nine years in a row. The Wegman's approach produces Contented Cows. If you look at the Employment Section of the Wegman's web site you'll see that the company credits its own employees with making them a great place to work. There's a hint for you!

So this is one half of my message to you as an employer: There is no big secret to learn about how to create a great working environment but there are some tough choices to make. My acquaintance from Wegman's was not referring to just how people were being compensated, although that must always be part of the equation. What she was talking about was treating people as assets not expense. Of course there is expense associated with employees and Wegman's is a retail grocery, so they keep track of all expense rigorously. But this is about seeing both sides of the balance sheet. I don't think this is too difficult for any of us to do but it does require that we make a conscious choice to operate in this fashion and not tolerate the bad actors who cannot make it across this bridge. Zero tolerance! Please remember, my message to "most people" contains an adamant reminder that the game of business must always be about results, so I am not in any way suggesting that there be a tolerance for poor performance either.

Being an employer and leader of an ongoing and successful enterprise today is tougher than it has ever been. Competition is everywhere, the folks we all need are in short supply, the character, values and even the colors of our workforces are changing at an increasing rate. If you didn't want to play a hard game you may just want to think about getting out now, because I don't believe things are going to get any easier soon. However, if what it means to you to be an employer or a professional manager is to play a game worth playing as well as you can, then this is your time!

This is the Age of Interdependence, not every man/woman for him/herself. As I said in my introduction to this book, the folks you are going to be looking for are not just waiting for the right time to start their own business, they are not going to start their own businesses. They could I suppose, but they really like what they do, they would just like some of the same opportunities and freedoms that have heretofore been reserved for the royalty of the enterprise, and now they know it is their responsibility to get what they want—if not from you, then from one of your competitors.

So the good news is there are still many people who are content to operate inside your organization. The bad news is they want some different things now, and they can get what they want. The first chapters of this book have been devoted to getting the herd of cows contented and to building the kind of workplace they want and are willing to help create. Remember, this is an interdependence I am looking to promote. It will take both sides of the relationship working together to make this work but there are distinct responsibilities for everyone involved.

I am going to suggest that the time has come for us as employers to commit to building a "culture of interdependence." It is time for us to invest, perhaps as an act of faith if nothing else. What I mean by a culture of interdependence comes down to two principles: that we recognize work as a sacred human pursuit—and that, fundamentally, we as humans thrive in environments where we can feel like we belong. Though they might not say it the same way, I believe it is the recognition of these two principles of people at work that sets folks like Max DuPree and Ralph Stayer apart from other business leaders.

I have personally met Ralph Stayer. It is not for me to judge if he is or is not a great business mind, but I could see that he was a great person, humble, aware of his shortcomings, but not apologetic. He had found a secret, and it wasn't sausage. He saw in his people a desire to play a key role in their own future and he set out to make the Johnsonville Sausage Company a place where people had a sense of belonging. I think Ralph Stayer also understands that people generally don't want more than they have contributed, but they do want to be rewarded consistently for what they have contributed. This adds mightily to a sense of belonging.

There are four main elements to the big idea of building a culture of interdependence. They all have to do with practices similar to those that would be followed by any asset manager:

- Knowing what we are trying to accomplish;
- Knowing what assets we have on hand and having a plan to optimize;

- Knowing the current state of performance of our assets; and
- Knowing what assets we are likely to need and having a plan for their acquisition

I think that we can learn a lot from the way some professional sports franchises build their teams. It has to do with the idea of *free agency*, which to me is only a fancy term for standing on your own two feet. So, let's look at it for what it has to show us in a real-world application. Long before free agency became something we needed to contend with in the business world, the world of professional sports was blown open by free agency. When this happened, some of the franchises were prepared and others have had their hands full ever since.

If we take professional football as one case in point, the Dallas Cowboys would seem to have had a wide advantage when free agency came on the scene. For years this franchise had built elaborate methods for understanding the talents it wanted to scout for and the talents they had on hand. My own belief is that this franchise held onto the old notion of loyalty too long and thereby lost a competitive advantage early in the new game, which was only regained when new ownership, committed to winning above all else, took over in the early 90's. So merely understanding the talent needs without an absolute commitment to winning is not enough to produce championship(s). Maybe one championship, but not several over time.

In baseball the early Yankee teams under the new ownership of George Steinbrenner appeared poised to take advantage of the full potential of free agency. Armed with a big bag of cash, Steinbrenner clearly set out to buy a world champion, and failed miserably until he learned the lesson that he needed more than simply talent, he needed an environment for that talent to flourish in as well. Under the field management of Joe Torre, a man who obviously respects his players as people, the Yankees have become perennial contenders in their sport for several years and often champions.

Finally, I have to mention my favorite of the recent past, a franchise which I believe for about a decade embodied the principles I am promoting. The San Francisco 49ers, under the ownership of Eddie De Bartolo and the management of Carmen Policy and the coaching of Bill Walsh come as close as I can imagine to the type of environment that produces champions over time, not every year but often. The objective of those teams was to win championships, each and every year. The manner in which the teams were constructed was intended to win championships. The salaries of the players, the length of contracts, the incentives offered, etc., were designed to attract talent that wanted, not just to play professional football, but to do whatever it took to win the championship ring. For about a decade the 49ers elevated the opportunity of working as a professional football player and focusing it on the Greater Good. The result, five Super Bowl Championships and many near misses in a ten year period with a wide variety of players who might have only been part of the organization for one or two seasons. But those days are gone too, and I suspect it is because someone forgot to say thank you when it would have made all the difference. The enemy of greatness in organizational performance is someone (or ones) thinking that they are more important than the Greater Good, and ceasing to honor the interdependence.

There really are only a few examples of sports franchises that have operated successfully in free agency. By successful I don't mean simply make money, but put a championship product on the field each and every outing. Some have tried to take the easy way out, some have tried to just hitch their wagon to a star, and others have tried to get to the top without making the all-out commitment to winning. And then there are many who have not really tried at all, and most of us who follow sports know who they are. Some owners are running a business and are trying to fill the seats, some others—a very few, are committed to winning championships. If you listen, they will sound the same, but if you look you will see they operate very differently.

So in my final analysis, what are the principles for operating successfully over time in this new economic reality?

- Employ people who are intrinsically motivated by what you are trying to accomplish;
- Employ people who currently possess skills and competencies that you really must have in your employ, and who are willing to continue to develop skills as needed in the interest of the Greater Good;
- Insist that your leaders take the long view and are accountable for the development of your human assets;
- Employ people who understand that yours is a collaborative environment; they must be willing to operate in that fashion and develop their collaborative skills;
- Make all your reward systems some combination of return to the individual for value produced and performance of the whole; and
- Create and maintain systems that allow people to grow professionally, and require that they take advantage of them.

These principles are the WHAT of building a Culture of Interdependence. I believe we have already saturated the WHY question. But don't you just hate those books that end without talking about the HOW? Just this once let's get that last question answered.

The initial and most profound answer to the HOW we are seeking is, "Yes!" It is all too common when topics of a risky nature arise to proffer the question of HOW as a sign of pragmatism or practicality, or worse yet, awareness of the "real world." Let me offer another interpretation of the question from a voice other than my own:

> *There is quite a depth to the question, "How do I do this?" that is worth exploring. The question is a defense against the action. It is a leap past the question of purpose, past the question of intentions, and past the drama of responsibility. The question "How"—more than any other question—looks for the answer outside of us. It is an indirect expression of our doubts.*
>
> Peter Block,
> *Stewardship: Choosing Service Over Self-Interest*

Is that the way we are going to end? With a philosophical *pie in the face*! I think pretty much that is the way we should end. Are there things you can do as an employer? Of course there are. In fact there are **many** things you can do. Unfortunately, at the end of the doing you still may not be where you want to be. What then? Will you continue, knowing that building "cultures of interdependence" is the right thing to do, that it is collaborative with the dharma of existence? If not, then let me end as Kurt Vonnegut ends his books and talks: "Thank you for your attention."

If you are ready to go on, ready to face the uncertainty of creation, then I have no guarantees to offer. I do have the same advice for you as I have for "most people"— focus on building relationships. But do not take on this challenge alone or only with members of management. Get everyone involved.

If we want people's intelligence and support, we must welcome them as co-creators. People only support what they create.

Margaret J. Wheatley,
"Innovation Means Relying on Everyone's Creativity," *Leader to Leader*, Spring 2001

There are some principles to utilize as foundational elements of the kinds for relationships you want to create. I am certain that I do not know them all, but here are a few, perhaps even some surprises:

Responsibility—Let it be known from day one that it is an expectation of membership, if you will, that every member will be responsible for their own development. Let it also be known to each person who has any responsibility for members' performance that they also have responsibility for their development, they are managers of development as well as performance.

Accountability—Accountability requires a person who will account. My firm belief is that the place to begin is by making someone in your organization accountable for the value of your human assets. This someone, whom we might call the Vice President of Human Assets or the Human Assets Officer, should have the same stature as any other senior executive.

Multilingualness—If it's not a word, I'll fall back on literary license to make this point anyway. Whoever is accountable for Human Asset Development must be able to speak at least two languages when it comes to human asset management, maybe more. The first is of course **the language of business**, valuing people in financial terms. This will take some thinking on the part of your financial folks but I cannot imagine it would be too hard. Other languages to be spoken by all would be *competency* and *talent*. These are relatively new languages in business but ones that do require rigor and literacy. Human Asset Managers and "members" should also all have some responsibility for understanding competence, the minimum requirements for the business to function; and they should have talent, an understanding of what your "members" could do if the competence was required—or alternatively, an understanding of what the business might be able to do if it availed itself of the talents of "members" and not merely asked for old notions of competency, i.e., what the business needed done at the moment. There are available today a variety of systems that can help your organization learn to speak both **competency** and **talent** and as importantly, to operationalize it.

Compassion—I haven't found a better definition than Thomas Merton's: "The whole idea of compassion is based on a keen awareness of the interdependence of all these living beings, which are all part of one another, and all involved in one another."

Spiritual Awareness—A sense of belonging, as in, "The organization has a spirit, it has an essence, it has a nature. It has ecology." Can we find ways to make sure we and our members stay tuned in? Is it strange to speak of spirituality and organizations in the same sentence? I do not think so, I have never thought so. I have lived my adult life in the presence of the possibility that eventually we would reach a point in time when the light of recognition would shine through the murkiness of the language of business and reveal that yes, they are economic enterprises, but the methodology of operation is at its heart a *human social system*. There is as much opportunity for the expression of the principles of democracy in our organizations as in our politics. Likely it will be the nurturing of this expression that takes this nation and its people to the next level of engagement, as citizens of the world community.

Ultimately, deep ecological awareness is spiritual or religious awareness. When the concept of the human spirit is understood as the mode of consciousness in which the individual feels a sense of belonging, of connectedness, to the cosmos as a whole, it becomes clear that ecological awareness is spiritual in its deepest essence.

Fritjof Capra, *The Web of Life*

So there you have it. As employers I have given us all a challenge. Together let's create a response that further fulfills the vision of those who created our nation. Now whatcha gonna do about it?

Helpful Resources

Training, Tools and Self-evaluation Instruments

For profiles on behavioral style and intrinsic motivators at
work:
*Target Training International, TTI performance Systems
Ltd., Scottsdale, Arizona,*
http://www.ttidisc.com
Tel: 800.869.6908

For help with understanding your natural instincts – what
work you will or won't like:
Kolbe International, Phoenix, Arizona,
http://www.kolbe.com
Tel: 800.642.2822

Special resource for entrepreneurs
The Strategic Coach, Toronto, Ontario,
http://strategiccoach.com
Tel: 800.387.3206

Tools for employers
Vitalsmarts Inc. Provo, Utah,
http://vitalsmarts.com
Tel: 800.449.5989

Contact the Author:
Vitalwork Inc., Rochester, New York,
http://www.vitalwork.com or mike@vitalwork.com
Tel: 585.387.9222

Suggested Reading
(categories somewhat arbitrarily
assigned by the author)

Practical skills for everyone at work:
*Crucial Conversations: Tools for Talking When the Stakes
are High,*
Joseph Grenny et al
McGraw-Hill

A must for employers:
Contented Cows Give Better Milk, Bill Catlette and
Richard Hadden
Saltillo Press

Thought-provoking:
Maslow on Management, Abraham Maslow
Wiley

*Waiting for the Mountain to Move: Reflections on Work
and Life,* Charles Handy
Jossey-Bass

Leadership and the New Sciences, Margaret Wheatley
Berrett-Koehler

*The Fifth Discipline: The Art and Practice of the
Learning Organization,*
Peter Senge
Currency

*The Empowered Manager, Positive Political Skills
at Work,* Peter Block
Jossey-Bass

Post-capitalist Society, Peter Drucker
HarperCollins

The Answer to How is Yes: Acting on What Matters,
Peter Block
Berrett-Koehler

Enlightening and thought-provoking:
The World is Flat: A Brief History of the 21st Century,
Thomas Friedman
Farrar, Straus and Giroux

Logical, thought-provoking and humbling:
Out of the Crisis, Edwards Deming
MIT Press

Deeply thought-provoking and inspirational:
Democracy in America, Harvey C. Mansfield and
Delba Winthrop
University of Chicago Press

Inspirational:
The Sermon on the Mount: The Key to Success in Life,
Emmet Fox
Harper San Francisco

The Hungry Spirit, Charles Handy
Broadway

Stewardship: Choosing Service Over Self Interest,
Peter Block
Barrett-Koehler

Leadership is an Art, Max DuPree
Dell

Practical and inspirational:
Making a Life, Making a Living, Mark Albion
Warner Books

Transformational:
On Becoming a Musical Mystical Bear, Matthew Fox
Paulist Press

Reinvention of Work: A New Vision of Livelihood for Our Times, Matthew Fox
HarperCollins

Freedom and Accountability at Work: Applying Philosophic Insight to the Real World, Peter Block
Pfeiffer

Educational:
Blur: The Speed of Change in the Connected Economy, Stan Davis and Christopher Myers
Warner Books

Now Discover Your Strengths, Marcus Buckingham and Donald O. Clifton
Free Press

Management Challenges for the 21st Century, Peter Drucker
HarperCollins

Reliable education on leadership development:
Any Issue of *Leader to Leader Journal*
Leader to Leader Institute and Jossey-Bass

A great read, a fun story of interdependence:
Life of Pi, Yann Martel
Harvest Books

Profound wisdom from a great American:
Living, Leading and the American Dream, John W. Gardner
Jossey-Bass

About the Author

Mike Cook is a founding partner of Vitalwork, providing leadership development services for middle managers and culture change processes for entire organizations. Mike's personal vision is to create tools that support individuals in mastering the skills of self-management.

He and his wife Pat Jackson live in Anacortes, Washington, and have four grown children and a granddaughter.

Mike can be found on the web at *www.vitalwork.com* or *www.thrivebook.com*.